Flags of the Fifty States
And Their
Incredible Histories

Randy Howe

Guilford, Connecticut
An Imprint of The Globe Pequot Press

To my parents, Sally and David Howe.
The nut doesn't fall far from the tree!

Copyright © 2004 by Randy Howe

Text design: Mary Ballachino
Flag design: Mario Fabretto

ISBN 1-58574-603-7
The Lyons Press is an imprint of The Globe Pequot Press

10 9 8 7 6 5 4 3 2 1

Printed in China

Library of Congress Cataloging-in-Publication Data

Howe, Randy.
   Flags of the fifty states and their incredible histories : the complete guide to America's most powerful symbols / Randy Howe.
      p. cm.
   ISBN 1-58574-603-7 (alk. paper)
   1. Flags--United States--States--History. I. Title.
   CR113.2 .H69 2002
   929.9'2'0973--dc21
                                        2002014799

Contents

Acknowledgments

I would like to offer personal thanks to my wife, Alicia Solis, and to my editor, Tom McCarthy, as well as Chris Mongillo, Kate Thompson, Kathryn Mennone, Dr. Peter "Flagman" Orenski, and Mr. Gettins, the teacher who breathed life into the past. This book would not have been possible without the help of the staff at the E.C. Scranton Memorial Library in Madison, Connecticut, and the many wonderful resources produced by each of the fifty states.

Introduction

There is a flag pole outside of just about every school in the United States. And an hour or two before the school day begins, a custodian faithfully unfolds an American flag and then reaches for the halyard. By the time the buses pull in, "Old Glory" is hanging high. It is the start of another day; another day added to the incredible history of our country.

When a school is fortunate enough to have a state flag, it is respectfully flown below the American flag. If a POW/MIA flag is also flown, you will see it beneath the other two. In the auditorium, with its bubble gum smell and Murphy's Oil shine, "Old Glory" stands to the left of the stage while the state flag stands to the right. You can almost hear the student body as it stands to pledge allegiance before the assembly.

Just as state flags must fly beneath the American flag, protocol dictates that they also must stand to the viewer's left. This arrangement provides our first glimpse of federalism, where powers not reserved for the federal government may be exercised by state governments. For example, state representatives have spent hours deciding what colors and symbols will best represent their state. In examining these legislative sessions, we learn how each individual state flag came to be. In this book, you'll notice that the states are not arranged alphabetically, but rather chronologically—in the order in which states were admitted, beginning with our first state, Delaware, and ending with our last, Hawaii. I've done this because, as you'll see, the influences of history often played a part in a flag's design.

Vexillology (the study of flags) is a relatively new word. It was added to the dictionary in 1959 and comes from the Latin word for flags, *vexillum*. Many consider Dr. Whitney Smith, director of the Flag Research Center in Winchester, Massachusetts, to be the founding father of modern vexillology. He has written books, encyclopedia entries, and articles on the subject and even started the North American Vexillological Association (NAVA), a group of flag

enthusiasts who have been meeting every year since 1967. The group's goal is to promote accuracy in flag knowledge and use. It was Flagman who taught me about NAVA and Dr. Smith.

I paid a visit to Flagman (*aka* Dr. Peter Orenski) to learn more about vexillology. Not only did Flagman, along with Dr. Mario Fabretto, provide the wonderful artwork in this book, he informed me of a recent NAVA survey. The end result was a listing of flags, from best to worst. In particular, the seventy-two flags of the American states and territories, along with the flags of the Canadian provinces, were ranked "based on their design qualities." This survey, the brainchild of NAVA member Ted Kaye, tells a lot about what we like and do not like in our flags. The winner was New Mexico, with its simple yet distinct Zía sun symbol on a field of yellow. The loser was Georgia, but that story deserves a closer look. The controversy that surrounds the former flag of Georgia, as well as the new flag (adopted in 2001), is just one of the things you will learn about as you read *Flags of the Fifty States and Their Incredible Histories.*

Although I have tried to let the flags speak for themselves, it is impossible to be completely objective. In the effort to be unbiased, and in the interest of sharing the opinions of other flag enthusiasts, I often refer to the state flags in the context of the "Great NAVA Survey of 2001." Another useful guideline when considering each of the fifty flags is Flagman's "Four Rules." These rules, borrowed from the flag contests that James Ferrigan conducted in the 1980s, relate to a flag's colors, simplicity, distinctness, and symbolism. Color and symbolism make the greatest impression on me when I look at a flag. Flagman, however, points out that simplicity and distinctness are also important. "The flag must be recognizable from fifty feet or on a one-inch lapel pin." I suppose I place emphasis on color and symbolism because I am drawn by a flag's meaning as well as its beauty. Beauty can actually be considered in three ways: aesthetically (based purely on its appearance), symbolically, and in a social/political/historical context. The standards for the NAVA survey did not include this last framework.

For budding vexillologists, it is important to be familiar with the five parts of the flag. First is the **canton**, or the upper left-hand corner. It is in the canton of "Old Glory" that you will find the fifty stars. Next is the **staff**, otherwise known as the flag pole. The part of the flag that flies closest to the staff is the **hoist side**. The opposite end of the flag, farthest from the staff, is the **fly** end. Between the hoist side and the fly end, but not including the canton, is the **field**. Among the fifty state flags, the most popular field color is dark blue; the same dark blue that we see behind the fifty stars of the American flag.

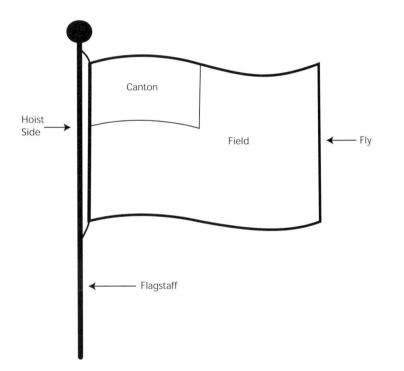

Look at your state flag. Compare it to the others you see in this book. Do you like it? Is it a muddled mess or is it aesthetically pleasing? Is the symbolism appropriate? Is it an accurate and respectful depiction of the history of your state? Or is there an image that better captures the people, animals, natural resources, and natural beauty of the place you call home? If you don't think so, change it. Write a letter to your state representative. You don't have to be a vexillologist to know that people are what made this country what it is, just as it was people who made each and every flag you are about to see. This is the story of those people.

Along with each flag, you'll find a map showing the state's location within one of four regions of the country, plus Alaska and Hawaii. The map above shows the various regions and how they all fit together within the continental United States.

Delaware

LIBERTY AND INDEPENDENCE

DECEMBER 7, 1787

Delaware

Admitted

December 7, 1787

Delaware has a rich history and strong ties to the roots of our nation. Henry Hudson is credited with discovering the "First State" in 1609, when he sailed into Delaware Bay under the flag of the Dutch East India Company. One year later, Captain Samuel Argall of Virginia honored his colony's governor, Baron De La Warr, by naming the bay, the river, and even a tribe of local Native Americans after him. Soon thereafter, De La Warr became Delaware.

Although only one battle of the American Revolutionary War took place on Delaware soil, it was at the Battle of Cooch's Bridge that the American flag, featuring thirteen stars for thirteen colonies, was flown for the first time. This was on September 3, 1777, ten years before Delaware would become the first state to sign the United States Constitution.

December 7, 1787, is another important date in our nation's history. Until that day, the federal government had been using the Articles of Confederation as a governmental guideline; they had yet to establish a balance of authority with the states. This balance, called "federalism," would soon be in place. In the summer of 1787, the Constitutional Convention had met in Philadelphia and agreed that, upon completion of the final draft of the Constitution, nine of the thirteen states would have to ratify the document before it could become official. Delaware was the first to do so, on December 7. This is why Delaware is often referred to as the "First State," and why the date December 7, 1787, appears prominently on its flag.

Delaware has three other nicknames. The "Blue Hen State" is a reference to the state bird and the roots of the name can be found in cockfights that took place during the American Revolutionary War. Soldiers from Kent County, fighting under Captain Jonathan Caldwell, brought the birds along for entertainment and subsequently earned the nickname. Legend also says that soldiers from the Delaware 1st Regiment were as ferocious as these fighting blue hens on the battlefield. Delawareans certainly celebrate their state bird with pride. Athletic teams from the University of Delaware display the name "Blue Hens" on their uniforms, and it is actually state law, outlined in Delaware Code Section 307, that the floor stand (or base) of the governor's flagpole be molded in the shape of a blue hen.

Thomas Jefferson once compared Delaware to a diamond. His reason: the state is small but very valuable. This explains another of Delaware's nicknames, the "Diamond State," as well as the presence of a diamond crest in the center of the state's flag. The diamond is buff, a goldish-beige that goes handsomely with the colonial blue (referred to by flag-makers as arno blue) field that makes up the flag's background. Buff and blue represent the colors of General George Washington's uniform as seen in an illustration in a United States Army publication.

The state's newest nickname is the "Small Wonder State." Delaware is one of the smallest states in the Union, both in population and in size. Upon completion of the 2000 census, Delaware's population was determined to be only 783,600 people. Delaware is so small that it is divided into just three counties. This makes for interesting politics, as the votes of each resident really do count.

Since ratifying the Delaware constitution in 1792, residents of the state have fought to defend freedom. The state song, "Our Delaware," ends with these words: "Liberty and Independence we will guard with loyal care/And hold fast to freedom's presence in our home state of Delaware." The phrase "Liberty and Independence" appears on the flag beneath the state seal. The symbols on the seal include a farmer with a hoe, representing the state's agricultural tradition, and a militiaman with a rifle, representing the role of citizens in defending freedom. Also present on the seal are a ship for coastal commerce and the shipbuilding industry, a sheaf of wheat and corn in another nod to agriculture, an ox for animal husbandry, and water representing the Delaware River.

The words "Liberty and Independence" were important enough

> **Delaware's official insect is the ladybug. These beetles are helpful in the garden, where they consume large quantities of plant-eating bugs. This might be why people consider them to be good luck!**
>
> **There are almost 4,000 species of ladybug worldwide and more than 350 in North America.**

Nicknames

"First State"
"Blue Hen State"
"Diamond State"
"Small Wonder State"

Motto

"Liberty and Independence"

Between 1763 and 1767, British astronomers Charles Mason and Jeremiah Dixon surveyed the land that would someday be known as the "Mason-Dixon Line." In the process, they set the western and southern borders of Delaware. These men had been hired to settle a land dispute between the Penn and Calvert families, who owned most of Pennsylvania and Maryland at the time. The Mason-Dixon Line, 244 miles in length, would gain fame during the Civil War; it was a popular reference point for differentiating between the South and the North.

to Delawareans that they chose them as the state's motto. This motto, approved by the General Assembly in 1847, was borrowed from the Society of the Cincinnati, an organization of people whose ancestors fought in the American Revolutionary War. The General Assembly adopted the current flag of Delaware, complete with date, diamond, and crest, on July 24, 1913.

Because Delaware was the first state to ratify the United States Constitution, the state's representatives get the honor of first position (i.e. the best seat in the house!) at important events such as the presidential inauguration. It is no surprise then that the date December 7, 1787, appears on the flag. Delawareans have every reason to be proud of their place in the history of the United States.

Pennsylvania

Pennsylvania

Admitted
December 12, 1787

While exploring the Delaware Bay in 1609, Henry Hudson discovered the land that would soon be called Pennsylvania. In this way, the early history of our second state is very similar to that of its neighbor to the south, Delaware. Their close ties would continue when the thirteen colonies banded together to form the United States of America. Once the American Revolutionary War was won, representatives of each state were sent to the Constitutional Convention to create an official document, a guideline that would last, these representatives hoped, for years to come. Five days after Delaware became the first state to sign the U.S. Constitution, Pennsylvania followed suit. Our constitutional democracy was now two states strong. The date was December 12, 1787.

In 1799, Pennsylvania's General Assembly approved the state's first official flag. Years later, on June 13, 1907, the General Assembly standardized and upgraded this flag. One new stipulation required that the blue field that serves as the background of the flag be changed so that it matches the blue of the American flag. On both flags, this blue is meant to signify loyalty and justice.

The Pennsylvania state flag consists of the official state seal embroidered on this field of blue. The seal includes a plow, sheaves of wheat, a cornstalk, and two horses, all in honor of the state's agricultural tradition; over thirty percent of Pennsylvania's land is considered rural. Encircling the seal are the words "State Seal of Pennsylvania." Inside the shield is an olive branch, a widely accepted symbol of peace, and a ship to represent commerce in the

> **Pennsylvania is known as the "Keystone State"; a keystone is the central, wedge-shaped stone in an arch—the stone that holds all others in place. At a party to celebrate Thomas Jefferson's presidential victory in 1801, Pennsylvania was referred to as "the keystone in the federal union." At that point, Pennsylvania was located centrally amid the thirteen states of the Union.**
>
> **Home to many colleges and universities, not to mention cities and historical sites, Pennsylvania certainly still lives up to its nickname.**

state. Philadelphia, Pennsylvania's largest city, has always been an important port for the import and export of goods.

Many of these images were borrowed from the seals of various Pennsylvania counties. The ship appeared on the seal of Philadelphia County, and the plow came from Chester County's crest. The sheaf of wheat appeared on the seal in Sussex County, Delaware, which was originally a part of Pennsylvania.

After the Revolutionary War, Americans wanted to be sure that the states would not lose control to their new federal government. Despite the fact that Pennsylvanian representatives were the second to sign the United States Constitution, state politicians and citizens felt the American president could not be given, let alone take, the same kind of unlimited power that the English kings had enjoyed. Reflective of this belief, Pennsylvania's state motto is "Virtue, Liberty, and Independence." It appears on the flag on a red ribbon beneath the two horses.

Pennsylvania is Latin for Penn's Woods. William Penn, who had been given control of the colony because of a debt owed to his father by King Charles II, named the state for its forestlands and for his father. It was in Pennsylvania that he established a safe haven for other followers of his religion, the Quakers, who believe that all people are equal in God's eyes. Many original Quaker meetinghouses still exist in Pennsylvania. There are no Quaker symbols on the state flag, however, reinforcing that American ideal of the separation of church and state.

> On June 14, 1777, the Continental Congress adopted the original United States flag, referred to as the "Stars and Stripes," in Philadelphia. June 14th has been known as "Flag Day" throughout the United States since the late 1880s.

Pennsylvanians have long displayed their state seal. During the Civil War, state regiments carried flags that were modeled after the United States flag; sewn onto the blue canton, where we see stars on the American flag, was the state seal.

An important part of the seal is the coat of arms. A number of changes were made to this coat of arms between 1778 and 1875, and different counties and institutions were employing different versions. This is why the state legislature appointed a commission to establish an official coat of arms in 1874. One year later, the commission adopted the coat of arms that had been designed by Caleb Lownes ninety-six years earlier. This same coat of arms is still in use today, meaning that Pennsylvania's most important symbol has gone virtually unchanged throughout the state's history.

Any student of American history knows that Philadelphia hosted the Constitutional Convention and is home to the Liberty Bell. What many people don't know, though, is that Philadelphia is also the birthplace of an American legend, Betsy Ross.

Elizabeth Griscom Ross, called "Betsy" by her friends, is said to have sewn the first flag of the United States of America. As the story goes, George Washington showed Betsy, a seamstress, a sketch of the "Stars and Stripes" (thirteen stars in a field of blue and thirteen red and white stripes) in church and asked if she would do this for her country. Betsy agreed, and the rest is truly history.

> **By name, Pennsylvania is officially a "commonwealth", as opposed to a "state." Kentucky, Massachusetts, and Virginia are also commonwealths. According to Merriam Webster's Collegiate Dictionary, a commonwealth is a republic (be it a nation, state, or any other political unit) "in which the supreme authority is vested in the people."**

New Jersey

On December 18, 1787, representatives from New Jersey signed the United States Constitution, making it the young nation's third state. It would not be until nearly one hundred twenty years later that New Jersey would adopt its current flag.

In the early 1600s, there was much exploration and settlement of the East Coast. Englishman Henry Hudson played a role in the early days of New Jersey's history. He first noticed the land while sailing the Delaware Bay for the Dutch East India Company; he then sailed up the coast toward New York and the Hudson River. The first Dutch settlements were on the land that would someday be Hoboken and Jersey City.

Once it was time for New Jersey to design a flag, the state followed a theme common to our nation's first states: the concept of liberty appears on New Jersey's flag in not one but two forms. The goddess Liberty stands to the left of the state seal, holding a staff topped with a liberty cap, a French hat that became a symbol for freedom during the French Revolution. The liberty cap appears on several of the fifty state flags. To the right of the state seal stands Ceres, the goddess of agriculture, holding a cornucopia. Cornucopias are often used to symbolize agriculture.

Liberty also appears on a ribbon of blue at the bottom of the flag. The word "Liberty" is scrolled beneath the goddess Liberty, while "Prosperity" appears below Ceres. The ribbon waves on a background of buff, or gold, in accordance with an 1896 decree of the New Jersey General Assembly: "General Washington, in General Orders dated Army Headquarters, New Windsor, New York, October 2nd, 1779, directed that the coats for such regiments should be dark blue, faced with buff." Although he issued the order from his

> **The legend of the Jersey Devil started in 1735 when Mother Leeds, a Pine Barrens resident frustrated with her thirteenth pregnancy wished the child to be a devil. The baby was just that and quickly fled to the Pines. Eyewitness reports from the early 20th century claim that the devil looks like a flying kangaroo with sharp fangs and claws. Today, the state's National Hockey League team goes by the name the Devils.**

camp in New York, it is said that General Washington made this decision while stationed in New Jersey, at Jockey Hollow, where he wintered before crossing the Delaware in his surprise attack on the British encampment. Jockey Hollow would later become the United States' first national park.

All three of New Jersey's neighboring states, Delaware, Pennsylvania and New York, followed Washington's color scheme when designing their flags. These colors have special importance, though, for New Jersey and New York, which were settled by the Dutch. Blue and buff are the colors that adorn the insignia of the Netherlands, and they are the colors that Henry Hudson flew as he sailed to the New World. Over the years, New York and Pennsylvania have adopted a darker shade of blue, while Delaware employs a lighter shade, called arno blue. New Jersyites now refer to their shade of blue as Jersey blue.

William Penn, founder of Pennsylvania, owned part of East Jersey for a while; the rest of New Jersey was actually a part of New York until the king of England named Lewis Morris governor of New Jersey in 1738. The Duke of York named the state to honor England's Isle of Jersey.

Since that time, New Jersey has made a name of its own. Some people know it as the home of Atlantic City, Princeton University, TV's "The Sopranos," or Bruce Springsteen, but these are just a few of the highlights. For example, the state's nickname, the "Garden State," refers to New Jersey's proud agricultural history. European settlers called New Jersey their "garden spot," and an important farming industry quickly cropped up here. New Jersey has always played host to dairy farms and horse farms, not to mention fields of crops that make their way to all of our dinner tables. The state seal sits in the center of the flag and features, in addition to Ceres and Liberty, three plows—yet another reference to New

> **In essence, New Jersey is a peninsula. After all, the state is completely surrounded by water on three sides. To the north is a fifty-mile stretch of land that borders on New York. Other than that, there is the Delaware River to the west, the Delaware Bay to the south, and the Atlantic Ocean to the east.**

Nickname

"Garden State"

Motto

"Liberty and Prosperity"

Jersey's farms. New Jersey's official animal is represented by a horse head above the seal. Despite the jokes about its extensive roadways, New Jersey is home to much soil that remains fertile today.

Although New Jersey is ranked forty-sixth among the states in terms of total area, its population stands at 8,414,350 (according to the 2000 census). This number is an 8.9 percent increase since the 1990 census and places New Jersey ninth among the fifty states. Since its discovery and settlement, New Jersey has grown and grown. Conveniently located for those who work in New York or Philadelphia, New Jersey is called home by people of all ethnic groups. Overpopulation and pollution remain a concern, but as long as residents, visitors, and elected officials continue to support local farming and natural areas like the Jersey Pine Barrens and Jockey Hollow National Park, images of agriculture will adorn the flag, satisfying Flagman's rule of symbolism (see Introduction).

> **In New Jersey it is against the law to pump your own gas. All gas stations are full service.**

> **Some states have an official State Fossil, but New Jersey is one of the few states to have a State Dinosaur. It is the Hadrosaurus, a twenty-eight-foot-tall creature whose bones were discovered in the town of Haddonfield.**

Georgia

Georgia

Admitted

January 2, 1788

Although Georgia is one of the original thirteen states, and the nation's fourth oldest, its flag is the most recent of all the fifty states. Adopted in 2001, this new flag tells an important American story of compromise and tradition, moderation and politics.

On January 2, 1788, Georgia ratified the United States Constitution and five years later Eli Whitney invented the cotton gin in Wilkes County, Georgia. Although the British had banned slavery upon founding the colony, the state's economic reliance on cotton would lead to an acceptance of the slave trade and the secession of Georgia from the Union once the Civil War began. Cotton is still farmed in Georgia today, and an image that some people associate with those darker days still exists in the form of the Confederate Battle Flag. It is this image that made Georgia's former state flag such a controversial issue.

On a field of blue, stretched across the bottom of the state's new flag, is a golden ribbon featuring five of the flags that flew over Georgia between 1776 and 2001. Like bookends, two United States flags surround three state flags of the past. On the far right is the current fifty-star version of "Old Glory"; on the far left is the thirteen-star "Betsy Ross" flag.

Georgians take pride in their state's place among the original thirteen colonies. Some Georgians also take pride in the Confederate Battle Flag. Second from the right on this ribbon is Georgia's former state flag. From 1956 to 2001, the Confederate Battle Flag was the most prominent aspect of this flag. At the height of the civil rights movement, people began to call for a change in the flag's design, citing the racism attached to the Confederate symbol. Protestors who saw hatred when they looked up at their state flag wanted either

> **Georgia lawmakers have taken action to preserve the history of their state. Section 50-3-5, the "Preservation of Confederate Flags," of the state statute reads: "The flags of the Georgia troops who served in the army of the Confederate States, and which have been returned to the state by the United States government, shall be preserved for all time in the capitol as priceless mementos of the cause they represented and of the heroism and patriotism of the men who bore them."**

a return to the pre-1956 flag or the adoption of a new flag. Their wish was finally granted on January 31, 2001, when Governor Roy Barnes signed House Bill 16 into law. In a compromise, this controversial flag still appears as one of the five on the golden ribbon at the bottom of the new flag. It sits second from the right, in between "Old Glory" and the state flag that flew from 1902 to 1956. Georgia's first state flag is also included on this ribbon, second from the left; this flag was adopted in 1879 and flew until 1902. Appropriately enough, the words "Georgia's History" appear above these five mini-flags.

Beneath the ribbon is the phrase "In God We Trust." Above the ribbon is the state seal, surrounded by thirteen stars for thirteen states. "State of Georgia" encircles the upper half of the seal, and "1776" appears at the bottom. Within the seal are three columns representing the three branches of government: legislative, judicial, and executive. A man with a drawn sword stands between two columns; the sword symbolizes Georgians' willingness to defend the Constitution ("Constitution" is written in an arc above the columns). Strung across the columns is a banner that features the three principles of the Constitution: "Wisdom," "Justice," and "Moderation."

> Georgia is America's tenth-most-populated state (8,186,453 people as of the 2000 census), but only the twenty-fourth-ranked state in terms of land (59,441 square miles). Atlanta, the state capital, is also Georgia's largest city.

If not simplicity, Georgia's new flag at least embodies moderation. Moderation, defined as temperance and self-control, is what the flag's designer, Cecil Alexander, is willing to accept for now. Although the NAVA (North American Vexillogical Association) flag survey found that Georgia's new flag ranks seventy-second out of the seventy-two flags from the United States and Canada, Mr. Alexander defends it on the grounds of moderation and compromise. In a recent edition of *Raven* (the official magazine of NAVA), Mr. Alexander expressed that some flags cannot, and should not, be judged aesthetically. With a history like Georgia's, he feels his flag must be addressed with "political and historical considerations" taken into account. In the least, he sees the flag as a step away from something far worse.

Nickname
"Peach State"

Motto
"Wisdom, Justice, Moderation"

Proponents of the new flag are concerned that negative press will fuel the fire of the Sons of Confederate Veterans, an organization whose members are "male descendents of any veteran who served honorably in the Confederate armed forces." If this group gains enough support, Georgia could see a return to the controversial flag that represented the state for nearly fifty years; a flag that some claim was adopted out of rebellion and racism. In the mid-1950s, the civil rights movement was gaining momentum as the Supreme Court made decisions like *Brown v. The Topeka Board of Education*, joining federal lawmakers in the fight against segregation and discrimination. Although the Confederate flag is often flown out of southern pride or to honor the Confederate dead, those who were fighting for desegregation in 1956 saw it as a banner of protest.

Governor Roy Barnes lost the 2002 election and one of the reasons cited by residents is the new state flag and how the public had no say in the change, via a vote. Governor-elect Sonny Perdue campaigned on a promise to return to the previous flag. Regardless, Mr. Alexander still feels that Georgia needed a new flag as soon as possible. The tension had to be eased. The pain had to be addressed. It would have been impossible to find a flag that made everyone happy; even harder than designing a flag that adhered to Flagman's Four Rules of color, simplicity, distinctness, and symbolism. Despite coming under fire from members of NAVA and many of his fellow Georgians, Mr. Alexander stands by his flag. He is proud of what he has done.

> **On average, 7,000 Coca-Cola products are being consumed each second of the day. In 1901, Atlanta's Dixie Coca-Cola Bottling Company changed its name to the Coca-Cola Bottling Company.**

Connecticut

By the end of 1788, the United States would count among its family eleven states. During that year, New Hampshire would become the ninth state to sign the United States Constitution, thereby ratifying this document as the guideline for our national government. (The Constitutional Convention had agreed that nine of the thirteen states would have to ratify the Constitution before it could become official.) In total, eight states would give their approval to the Constitution that year, thus gaining entry into the Union. Connecticut was one of these states.

On January 9, 1788, Connecticut became the fifth colony to attain statehood. More than one hundred years later, the state's governor, O. William Coffin, decided that it was finally time for Connecticut to have an official state flag and proposed the idea to the General Assembly, which appointed a special committee. Ultimately the state's unofficial flag would simply be standardized (and not redesigned), but it took another two years before this flag was adopted.

The state flag's design, borrowing from a memorial created by the Anna Warner Bailey Chapter of the Daughters of the American Revolution, features a Latin motto printed across a white banner. "*Qui Transulit Sustinet,*" scrolled in navy blue, translates to "He Who Transplants Still Sustains." The colonists were transplants from the Old World, intent upon making the New World their home. When pilgrims from Europe crossed the Atlantic Ocean, and when colonists from Massachusetts moved south, and arrived in Connecticut, a tradition known as the "American Dream" was born. The defeat of the British in the American Revolutionary War, topped by the creation of the new Constitution for the new nation, gave Americans faith in their sustainability.

George W. Bush, the forty-third president of the United States, was born in New Haven on July 6, 1946. Both he and his father (George Herbert Walker Bush, the forty-first president) attended Yale University, the state's finest college. George W. Bush is the first president to have twins; one of his daughters, Barbara, also attends Yale.

The flag's white banner, trimmed in silver, is complemented by a shield that is centered in a field of azure blue. The shield is actually the official state seal of Connecticut, with a touch of gold added in. The flag, as described by the statute agreed upon by the state's General Assembly, is to be made of silk.

On the shield are three grapevines, each of which bears fruit. Just as nearly all Americans are transplants from somewhere else, the flag's three bunches of purple grapes represent those pilgrims who chose Connecticut as a home in the early 1600s. Since grapevines can be transplanted, they are a perfect symbol for Connecticut: a nod to a state history that runs as deep as the history of the country itself.

The state's nickname is proof of just how far back Connecticut's history runs. Although also referred to as the "Nutmeg State," Connecticut is best known as the "Constitution State." In the late 19th century, local historian John Fiske wrote that Connecticut's *Fundamental Orders of 1638–39* was "the first written constitution known to history that created a government and it marked the beginning of American democracy." Although this claim has been questioned by other historians, the Connecticut General Assembly saw fit to dub its state the "Constitution State" in 1959.

> In 1978, "Yankee Doodle" was made Connecticut's official song in recognition of the state's history as one of the original thirteen colonies.

The *Fundamental Orders* marked Connecticut's beginning as a commonwealth. Just before the acceptance of this document, the Reverend Thomas Hooker remarked that, "The foundation of authority is laid in the free consent of the people." And, he added, "As God has given us liberty let us take it." The colonists felt no allegiance to England and sought an independent government, even if this government was to be ruled by the church. In America's early days, religion and politics went hand in hand. For example, New Haven was settled by Puritans from the Massachusetts Bay Company, and until it was made a part of the colony of Connecticut in 1665, was its own colony. This New Haven colony, incidentally, included several towns on Long Island. This was not uncommon as East Hampton and Southampton were also a part of the Connecticut

Nicknames

"Nutmeg State"
"Constitution State"

Motto

"He Who Transplants Still Sustains"

colony. The New Haven colony was ruled by theocracy, meaning that the government leaders were also religious leaders. This was long before the United States Constitution and the advent of the separation of church and state.

Nathan Hale is the official hero of Connecticut. When the Revolutionary War began, Hale was a twenty-one-year-old schoolteacher. He volunteered to fight against the Red Coats and, after the Battle of Boston, volunteered to become a spy. He entered British territory on Long Island under the guise of being a simple school-teacher. Unfortunately, the British caught him and hanged him without a trial. Before his death, Hale made one of the most memorable statements in American history: "I only regret that I have but one life to lose for my country." Although Hale did not survive the Revolutionary War, the country did. The United States of America was free to rule itself; ready to develop a Constitution that guaranteed individual and states rights; ready to roll out the welcome mat to immigrants the world over.

Qui transtulit sustinet!

> **All three rock types—sedimentary, igneous, and metamorphic—are found in Connecticut. The last Connecticut glacier melted a mere 15,000 years ago.**

> **In 1614, Dutch explorer Adriaen Block discovered the Connecticut River (the colony was named after the river). Block would sail up the East Coast, also discovering the land that would someday be Rhode Island. Block Island, off the coast of Connecticut and Rhode Island, was named in his honor.**

Massachusetts

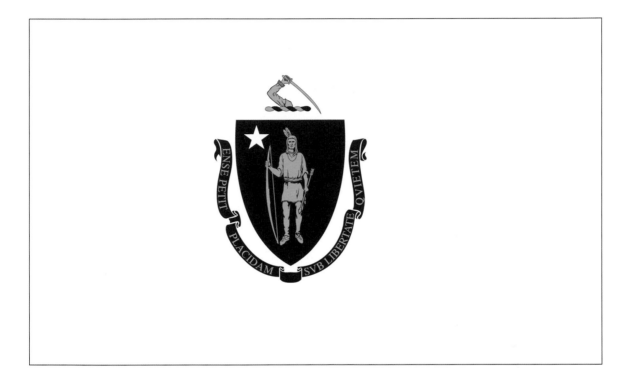

Admitted

February 6, 1788

On February 6, 1788, the Commonwealth of Massachusetts signed the United States Constitution and became a state. Being a commonwealth (also called a republic) means that Massachusetts is governed by its people. This term, which can be traced to the second draft of the Massachusetts constitution, written by John Adams in 1780, was meant to further distinguish our democracy from the monarchy in England. Kentucky, Pennsylvania, and Virginia are also commonwealths. In essence, this is just a name: there is no real difference between a commonwealth and a state.

Massachusetts adopted its state flag in 1915 and amended it slightly in 1971. It was the first state to employ a plain white field on its flag, thus drawing attention to the blue shield featured in its center. This shield's most prominent feature is a Native American from the Algonquin tribe. (Surprisingly, the figure does not represent the Massachuset tribe, which, like the Algonquin, lived in what is now known as New England.) The name *Massachuset* means "a large hill place." The names of many Massachusetts towns have their roots in either Native American words or cities in Great Britain.

Massachusetts owes its survival to the natives of the land. It was the Massachuset tribe who taught the pilgrims how to farm the land and survive the brutal winters and who shared the first Thanksgiving with the European settlers. Not only was the Massachusetts state flag the first to use a white background, it was the first to feature a Native American.

The Algonquin holds a bow in one hand and an arrow in the other. The arrow is pointing downward, symbolizing peace. The image is drawn completely in gold, from the arrow to the shirt to the moccasins. Around the bot-

> **The Franklin Public Library was America's first free public lending library. In 1778, Benjamin Franklin donated books to the town (which had just changed its name from Exeter to Franklin in his honor) for use by the citizens, instead of donating the bell that town officials had requested. In explaining his actions, Franklin said that "sense" was preferable to "sound." His books are still on display at the library.**

tom half of the seal is a blue ribbon with the Latin motto *"Ense petit placidam sub libertate quietem,"* or "By the sword we seek peace, but peace only under liberty." Some might argue that the image above the shield, and not the Algonquin, is the most notable aspect of the flag: it is a muscular white arm and hand grasping a broadsword. This image is meant to reinforce the state motto: we will be peaceful as long as our freedom is not in jeopardy. Unfortunately, the Native Americans who had welcomed the pilgrims to Massachusetts later saw the sword.

These controversial images come from the state's seal, which was adopted by Governor John Hancock in 1780 and made official by the Massachusetts General Court on June 4, 1885. When the seal was applied to the flag, the Latin phrase for "Seal of the Republic of Massachusetts" was dropped so as to avoid cluttering the flag— thus abiding by at least one of Flagman's rules: a flag should be distinctive (as was described in the Introduction). The five-point star, seen above the Algonquin's right shoulder, is white on the flag and silver on the state seal.

Massachusetts is nicknamed the "Bay State" in tribute to the early settlements on Cape Cod, Massachusetts Bay, and Buzzards Bay. The nickname is mentioned in Arthur March's state song, "All Hail to Massachusetts": "All hail to grand old Bay State, the home of the bean and the cod." Massachusetts is also known as the "Baked Bean State," "Old Colony State" (a reference to that first colony at Plymouth), and the "Puritan State."

Like other New Englanders, the citizens of Massachusetts are called "Yankees." This name goes back to the Revolutionary War, when the Yankees fought the Red Coats of Great Britain. Ironically enough, the state's beloved baseball team is the Boston Red Sox, while the hated rivals from New York are the Yankees. The finest player to ever wear the Red Sox uniform was Ted

> **Four American presidents were born in Massachusetts: John Adams (October 30, 1735), his son, John Quincy Adams (July 11, 1767), John Fitzgerald Kennedy (May 29, 1917), and George Herbert Walker Bush (June 12, 1924).**

Nicknames

"Bay State"
"Baked Bean State"
"Old Colony State"
"Puritan State"

Motto

"By the Sword We Seek Peace, but Peace Only Under Liberty"

Williams, the last man to bat .400 at the major league level. Today a tunnel beneath Boston Harbor is named for him.

Massachusetts's population has ranked thirteenth in the nation for the last two censuses. As of 2000, the population is 6,349,097. All of these citizens are still governed under the original state constitution, adopted in 1780.

A good part of Massachusetts's economy centers around tourism. In addition to the city of Boston and the vacation haven of Cape Cod, offbeat highlights include Worcester's American Sanitary Plumbing Museum and Salem's Witch Dungeon Museum. You won't find any toilets or witches on the state's flag, just like you won't find any symbols of manufacturing or agriculture, despite the fact that Massachusetts's economy has long relied on both. In particular, the state is known for its seafood and cranberries. The textile mills at Lowell should also be given historical consideration. They employed some of the first single women in the country to leave home. Instead of staying on the family farm, these women made the bold decision to move to the city in pursuit of income and independence. An American endeavor, for sure.

> "Johnny Appleseed" is the official folk hero of Massachusetts. John "Johnny Appleseed" Chapman was born on September 26, 1774, and his practice of planting apple trees, from New England to the Midwest, earned him his name. Chapman died in 1845; legend has it that it was the first time he had ever been sick.

Maryland

Maryland

Admitted

April 28, 1788

Maryland was admitted to the Union on April 28, 1788. The seventh of the original thirteen colonies-turned-states to sign the United States Constitution, Maryland was the fourth to do so that year. This was a good sign for the federal government; as soon as two more states ratified the Constitution it would become official.

One of the first states to fly its own flag, Maryland has known only one. This flag has gone unchanged since its official adoption in 1904; it is a flag that Maryland has known much longer than that. Reflecting a history that reaches back across the Atlantic Ocean, the flag's two distinct designs are borrowed from the family coat of arms of the first Lord Baltimore, George Calvert. His son, Cecil, second Lord Baltimore, founded the colony of Maryland in 1634. The state's largest city is named in honor of the Baltimores.

Repeated in the upper left and lower right cantons (or corners) of the flag is the Calvert family coat of arms. The vertical bars of black and gold have always been accepted as the state colors. In the other two cantons sit a red-and-white design that was borrowed from the Crossland coat of arms in honor of George Calvert's mother, who was a Crossland. This coat of arms' most interesting feature is "a Greek cross with arms terminating in trefoils" as described in Maryland statute 1.02. The trefoils appear at the end of each of the four arms of the cross, rounded like the club symbol you would find in a deck of cards. A cross with such rounded ends, or buds, is called a cross bottony.

Maryland adopted the Calvert and Crossland coats of arms as the official state seal in 1854. The state seal was then placed on a background of blue whenever it was flown on a flag. As the Civil War loomed, however, the

> **Maryland, named for Queen Henrietta Maria of England, is known as the "Free State" for its decision to fight slavery. But its more commonly used nickname is the "Old Line State." Legend has it that George Washington once complimented Maryland's soldiers. These troops, who fought courageously during the Revolutionary War, were called the "Maryland Line."**

divisive nature of the seal reflected the debate that Maryland's citizens were having over slavery and secession.

The black and gold of the Calvert family, known today as "Maryland colors" or "Baltimore colors," came to symbolize those loyalists who wished to remain a part of the Union. When Abraham Lincoln was elected president and it became obvious that Maryland would not vote to secede, Confederate sympathizers in Maryland rallied around the red and white of the Crossland family. These colors appeared on Confederate flags and banners, and Confederate soldiers from Maryland used the cross bottony shape to identify their birthplace. In the North, anyone seen wearing the red and white of the Crossland family was arrested. Even though these two family designs had yet to be accepted as the state's official flag, they carried enough meaning to play a role in the fissure that was running right through the middle of the country.

It wasn't until after the Civil War that the two coats of arms began to appear together again. The unofficial state flag became a symbol of the healing that was taking place as soldiers from the Union and the Confederacy began to live as neighbors again. The earliest appearance of a banner with the four-quadrangle de-

> **If you look at a map, you will see that the Chesapeake Bay nearly splits Maryland in half. The Bay was carved out during the last Ice Age and is fed by one hundred fifty rivers and tributaries.**

sign of the Calvert and Crossland families was in 1880, at a parade to celebrate the one-hundred-fiftieth anniversary of the city of Baltimore. The flag was carried by the Fifth Regiment of Maryland's National Guard and was flown in 1888 at a ceremony at Gettysburg. These early appearances helped make the design popular with all of the state's citizens, especially since soldiers who had fought in the Civil War were not only neighbors again, their sons were serving together in the National Guard and would be fighting, side by side, in the Spanish-American War of 1898.

In the years that followed the flag's formal adoption in 1904 came rules of protection and protocol. For example, according to a 1945 Maryland law, "Only a gold cross bottony may be used as an ornament on the top of a

flagstaff that carries the Maryland flag."
(Other states, like Maine and Delaware, have similar laws.) As described in the *Annotated Code of Maryland,* protocol states that, "The Secretary of State is required by law to present a State flag to the family of any firefighter or police officer killed in the line of duty. The flag

In "The Great NAVA Survey of 2001," Maryland's unique design earned its flag fourth place out of seventy-two flags!

is to be presented to the family of the deceased firefighter or police officer by the State senator of the legislative district in which the deceased resided."

Despite its complex design, the Maryland state flag ranked fourth in the NAVA (North American Vexillogical Association) flag survey. It is distinct while offering a reminder of the past, a nod to the state's roots with bold colors and a rich design. It is the only flag that Maryland has ever known.

Maryland was the first state to have an official sport. Jousting, originally a medieval contest between two men on horseback, was named the state sport in 1962. Jousting was popular in Maryland in the 1800s.

South Carolina

Admitted

May 23, 1788

It was during the 1500s that Spanish and French explorers arrived in Carolina. However, it was the British that gave the colony its name. Beginning in 1670, when the first permanent British settlement was established, they referred to the colony by this name: Carolina. The name was a tribute to England's king, Charles I. ("Carolus" means Charles in Latin.) In 1710, the British decided to split Carolina into two colonies and South Carolina and North Carolina were established.

It took more than one hundred years for a European settlement to survive. It was not until 1670 that an English settlement, somewhere near present day Charleston, was able to endure. Settlers soon followed, sailing to the New World to farm the land. They built plantations near the coast and grew rice and indigo. This helped to make South Carolina one of the wealthier colonies.

In 1775, colonial leaders asked Colonel William Moultrie to design a flag for the troops of South Carolina. The only point of reference he had was a flag that had been raised ten years earlier to protest the Stamp Act, an English tax that many of the increasingly independent colonists thought of as unfair. "No taxation without representation!" was the motto of the day and related, in part, back to these British stamps. Even though the Stamp Act was overturned, the colonies were on a collision course with Great Britain. And when that collision happened, South Carolina once again needed a symbol to fly in

In the NAVA flag survey, voters showed their overwhelming support for the flag of South Carolina. The palmetto flag came in tenth out of seventy-two flags. No wonder it has gone unchanged since 1860!

the face of the enemy. Moultrie chose a blue field that not only matched that earlier flag but was also the color of the uniform of the South Carolina militia. He then added a silver crescent moon, reminiscent of the moon seen on the front of the soldiers' caps. The colony that was soon to be called a state now had a flag.

Of the one hundred and thirty-seven Revolutionary War battles that took place on South Carolina soil, one, in particular, stands out. On July 28, 1776, British warships launched an ill-fated attack on the American fort on Sullivan's

Island. The palmetto logs that served as the fort's walls proved impenetrable. The British cannonballs either sank into the soft wood or bounced right off. The victorious commander of the fort was none other than the flag-designing Colonel Moultrie, who now owed a debt of gratitude to the palmetto.

Ironically, it took another forty-eight years before this tree took center stage on South Carolina's state flag. The Sabal (or "Cabbage") Palmetto was named the official state tree in 1939 and today, South Carolina is known as the "Palmetto State."

On the flag, the Palmetto stands independently beneath the crescent moon and this is reflective of the state's rebellious stance during the "War Between the States." On December 20, 1860, South Carolina seceded from the Union and the blue and silver palmetto flag flew with new meaning. Just as they had embraced their rebellious status in the Revolutionary War, South Carolinians gave their full support to the Confederacy during the Civil War. And just as they had known only one flag throughout their history, South Carolinians knew only one way to defend their beliefs: fiercely; tough like the wood of the palmetto.

After the palmetto was added to the flag, the legislators in South Carolina saw fit to adopt it as the official flag of the state. At the time, many viewed it as their national flag because statehood was a thing of the past as far as South Carolinians were concerned. But the Civil War ended and the North and South were reunited. It was hard for South Carolina to recover. They had lost nearly one-fifth of their white male population and their once glorious economy was in ruins. They continued to fly the flag proudly, though, and the General Assembly demonstrated this pride when, in 1899, they denied a request to change the field of the flag from blue to royal purple. This means that the flag, which predates by only forty-two years the birth of South Carolina's Strom Thurmond, the United States Senate's longest-serving member, has looked the same since 1860.

Some aspects of South Carolina have changed with the years. As of 2000, the state's population had become quite diverse. The percentage of the population that is African-American is much higher than the average nationwide (29.5 percent versus 12.3 percent). Some aspects of life have remained the same, or at least similar, to those early days of statehood. Instead of rice and

The right to burn the American flag enrages many people. While one side of the debate stands on the grounds of freedom of speech, the other draws the line at patriotism. In South Carolina there is no debate: anyone who mutilates, injures or desecrates the flag can be fined up to $100 or imprisoned for up to thirty days. A judge may also see fit to punish the defendant with a fine *and* imprisonment.

indigo, South Carolina's farms now grow tobacco, melons, peas, peaches, peppers, onions, and tomatoes. Tourism has also become important to the state's economy. In particular, Hilton Head, Charleston, and Kiawah Island are favorite vacationing spots.

The years after the Civil War, referred to as Reconstruction, were difficult for South Carolina's residents, black and white alike. By making changes in their agricultural priorities, by looking at the state's resources and rethinking how to use them, South Carolinians were able to recover economically. This brings to mind one of the state mottoes, "Animis Opibusque Parati" or "Prepared in Mind and Resources." Just as South Carolinians, independent yet flexible, have been well represented by the palmetto, it would seem that their motto is also appropriate.

New Hampshire

Admitted

June 21, 1788

When New Hampshire ratified the United States Constitution, it was a significant historical event. The year was 1788, and New Hampshire was the ninth state to sign the document that would serve as the framework for our federal government; their approval made the Constitution official. The framers of the Constitution had decided that nine of the thirteen states would be needed for ratification. New Hampshire's flag features nine stars to commemorate the state's place in American history.

New Hampshire attained statehood on June 21, 1788, and since 1909 has flown the same flag. Another important year in New Hampshire's history was 1920; it was in this year that this tiny state became the most important whistle-stop for U.S. presidential candidates. As tradition would have it, New Hampshire has been the first state to hold a presidential primary ever since. Every four years, the media swarm to a town called Dixville Notch to learn the frontrunner for the most powerful governmental position in the world. New Hampshire's is the first of several primaries leading up to the actual election, but more times than not, the winner of the New Hampshire primary has landed in the White House.

New Hampshire's flag is ordinary in that it employs the basic blue field and state seal. Almost half the states use a blue field, and one of the opinions that was proved by the "Great NAVA Survey of 2001" is that the use of a state seal on a flag is not necessarily aesthetically pleasing. New Hampshire's flag was sixty-third out of seventy-two flags, but is able to distinguish itself in that it features the classic image (both symbolic and historically appropriate) of a warship on its seal. The *Raleigh* was a U.S. frigate built in Portsmouth, New Hampshire, and used to battle the British during the Revolutionary War.

New Hampshire made Civil Rights Day a state holiday in 1991. In turn, the state eliminated its traditional Fast Day. Fast Days were once popular in New England; people fasted to avoid crop failures, plagues, and earthquakes. In 1894, Massachusetts replaced Fast Day with Patriot's Day, but in 1899, politicians in New Hampshire made Fast Day a legal holiday.

Flying proudly from the stern of this ship is the American flag. During that war, the U.S. flag had only thirteen stars in the blue canton: thirteen stars for thirteen states. The *Raleigh* was the first ship to fly the U.S. flag at sea and was one of thirteen warships commissioned by the Continental Congress. On the seal, the ship appears on land, still on its stocks (to represent shipbuilding), with a stretch of granite in the foreground. Beyond the ship, the sun is rising in brilliant hues of yellow and gold.

New Hampshire played an important role in the country's fight for independence. The state's people protested the Stamp Act, which was passed by British Parliament in 1765 and required that a tax be paid on official documents. And it was soldiers from New Hampshire who first stole gunpowder and ammunition from British troops several weeks before the Battles of Lexington and Concord. It's a lesser-known fact that at the Battle of Bunker Hill, New Hampshire's one thousand soldiers outnumbered the combined troops from Massachusetts and Connecticut.

On New Hampshire's seal, "1776," the year of independence, is inscribed in gold beneath the image of the *Raleigh*. Continuing in a circle around the warship are the gold embroidered words "Seal of the State of New Hampshire." Surrounding the seal are nine stars and a laurel wreath, also done in gold.

New Hampshire did not officially adopt its flag until 1909. It has been altered only once since then, in 1931, when the state's seal was changed. Apparently, artists were taking liberties with the *Raleigh*. Some versions of the seal even included barrels of rum on the deck. This was remedied, and the seal was standardized.

> **Author John Irving was born in Exeter, New Hampshire, and attended Phillips Exeter Academy as well as the University of New Hampshire. He has characterized the state in several books, including *A Prayer for Owen Meany* and *The Hotel New Hampshire*. In *Owen Meany*, a granite quarry is the setting for several important scenes.**

Nicknames

"Granite State"
"Mother of Rivers"
"White Mountain State"
"Switzerland of America"

Motto

"Live Free or Die"

New Hampshire has an official state tartan (a plaid design used to identify Scottish families). The colors in the tartan all have meaning: purple is for the state's bird (the purple finch) and flower (the purple lilac), green is for the forests, black is for the granite mountains, white is for the snow, and red represents all of the state's heroes. The tartan became official in 1995.

Three years after pilgrims arrived at Plymouth Rock, New Hampshire's first settlement was established. Using an English land-grant, Captain John Mason sent Scotsman David Thomson, along with two divisions of soldiers and two English fishermen, Edward and Thomas Hilton, to establish a fishing colony along the Piscataqua River. In later years the state achieved other notable firsts. In 1774, New Hampshire was the first colony to declare its independence from England. Two years later, the *Raleigh* was commissioned and built (in only sixty days!). New Hampshire went on to become the first state to adopt its own constitution, and of course the state played an extremely significant role in ratifying the Constitution. It seems fitting, then, that New Hampshire is the first state to host a presidential primary every four years.

New Hampshire has four nicknames. The state is speckled with granite, thus the name the "Granite State." New Hampshire is also referred to as the "Mother of Rivers," because several rivers, including the Connecticut, the Winnipesaukee, and the Merrimack, originate here. In all, New Hampshire boasts over 40,000 miles of rivers and streams. Two other state nicknames are the "White Mountain State," for the White Mountain Range, and the "Switzerland of America," also a reference to the state's many peaks.

Virginia

37

Virginia

Admitted
June 25, 1788

T he Commonwealth of Virginia was originally named for England's Queen Elizabeth I (called the "Virgin Queen" because she never married), but Virginia's flag demonstrates strong patriotic feelings. "Virginia" appears on the flag, as does the state motto: "*Sic Semper Tyrannis*," which means "Thus Always to Tyrants." (Although Virginia, like Kentucky, Massachusetts, and Pennsylvania is a commonwealth, the secretary of the commonwealth's website refers to all symbols as "state symbols," except for the "seal of the commonwealth.") When Virginia chose this motto and designed its state flag, England was that tyrant.

There are two figures on the flag. One is a woman, the Roman goddess "Virtus," or Virtue. She is dressed as an Amazon warrior, in a light blue robe, and is meant to represent Virginia. Sword in one hand, spear in the other, she stands victoriously over the tyrant; her foot is planted firmly on his chest, exemplifying her dominant position. The tyrant is a man, also dressed as a warrior. Beside him, knocked to the ground, is his crown. He is still holding onto a scourge (a whip) and a chain. "Thus Always to Tyrants" is a warning; Virginia and the United States would treat any oppressor in just such a manner.

These words and images appear in a white circle, fringed with red Virginia creepers and green leaves, on a field of blue. As with so many other state flags, the words and images are borrowed from the official seal, which Virginia's Constitutional Convention adopted on July 5, 1776, one day after our young nation's Independence Day. This date also means that Virginia had an official seal before it was even considered a state.

Since then the seal has not changed but, as in New Hampshire, official rules have been laid out for its preservation. In 1930, a committee prepared an "accurate and faithful description of the great seal of the Commonwealth, as it was intended to be by Mason and Wythe and their associates." George Wythe, the seal's main designer, borrowed several of the images from Roman mythology. George Mason was a patriotic leader who played a number of roles at Virginia's Constitutional Convention. In addition to helping design the seal, he wrote a declaration of rights that was used as a template by many other states. Mason's words also influenced fellow Virginian Thomas Jefferson when he wrote the Declaration of Independence. Mason would later take part in the Constitutional Convention, in 1787. He refused, along with

Patrick Henry, to sign the United States Constitution until the Bill of Rights was added. Today, one of Virginia's universities is named in George Mason's honor.

In addition to George Mason University and the University of Virginia, Virginia is also home to Old Dominion. This school's name is a reference to the state's nickname, the "Old Dominion State," which comes from the days of King Charles II. In 1663, the king was responsible for turning Virginia into England's first colony in the New World. The dominion that Virginia had been added to included Ireland and Scotland. Although it has been a very long time since England dominated the United States, "Old Dominion" still stands as the state nickname today.

> **The majority of people in the United States live on or near the East Coast. According to the 2000 census, more than half of America's 287,671,785 people live within five hundred miles of Virginia.**

Virginia boasts several other fine universities and colleges. James Madison University, named for the native son and president, is in Harrisonburg. Washington and Lee University pays homage to Virginia's American and Confederate roots (Richmond was the capital of the Confederacy, and more Civil War battles were fought in Virginia than in any other state) by combining the names of George Washington and Robert E. Lee. And the College of William and Mary, opened in 1694, is the oldest college in Virginia and the second oldest in the United States, behind Harvard. Thomas Jefferson attended the College of William and Mary.

Virginia's lesser-known nickname is the "Mother of Presidents." Eight United States presidents were born here: George Washington, the aforementioned Thomas Jefferson, James Madison, James Monroe, William Henry Harrison, John Tyler, Zachary Taylor, and Woodrow Wilson.

Just as our nation has a Pledge of Allegiance, many states have adopted pledges for their flags. Virginia has designated the following as its official salute to the flag: "I salute the flag of Virginia, with reverence and patriotic devotion to the 'Mother of States and Statesmen,' which it represents—the 'Old Dominion,' where liberty and independence were born."

Motto
"Thus Always
to Tyrants"

Virginia   39

Virginia attained statehood on June 25, 1788. It was the seventh state to join the Union that year, and the tenth overall. Seventy-three years later, in 1861, Virginia adopted its first official state flag. This was during the tumultuous times of the Civil War. The Virginia State Convention passed an ordinance that simply made official the flag that had been raised for years. This was done so that Virginia troops would have a reminder of home and of what they were fighting for. Richmond was the capital of the Confederacy and is still the capital of the state today.

> **The Chesapeake Bay is an estuary (an extension of the ocean at the lower end of the river) where fresh and salt water mix. The Bay is almost 200 miles long.**

New York

41

Admitted

July 26, 1788

When French sculptor Frédéric Auguste Bartholdi visited America in 1871, he thought that Bedloe's Island in New York Harbor would be the perfect home for his statue. Officially named *Liberty Enlightening the World*, the Statue of Liberty was first erected in Paris and then shipped to New York, where President Grover Cleveland dedicated it on October 28, 1886. In 1924, it was declared a National Monument, and in 1956, Bedloe's Island was renamed Liberty Island.

The Statue of Liberty still stands guard over New York Harbor today, glancing seaward with a ledger cradled in her left hand and the torch of freedom raised high in her right. Engraved on the ledger is "July IV, MDCCLXXVI," or July 4, 1776. This gift from France has become the quintessential symbol of America and of America's most important port city. The French wished to recognize the friendship of the two countries, along with the shared histories of the American and French Revolutions. In particular, democratic rule for the people, by the people, was the common theme when the American and French citizens overthrew the ruling monarchies. France's grand gift, the work of the aforementioned Frédéric Auguste Bartholdi, was intended to be an antimonarchy symbol as well as a statement against slavery. The statue's name is borrowed from the goddess Liberty.

> **Virginia may lay claim to almost one-fifth of the U.S. presidents, but New York gave birth to these famous people: Kareem Abdul-Jabbar; Lucille Ball; Humphrey Bogart; James Cagney; Sean "P Diddy" Combs; Aaron Copland; Tom Cruise; Sammy Davis, Jr.; George Eastman; Millard Fillmore; Henry Louis Gehrig; Sarah Michelle Gellar; George Gershwin; Jackie Gleason; Chamique Holdsclaw; Washington Irving; Henry James; Billy Joel; Vince Lombardi; Chico, Groucho, Harpo, and Zeppo Marx; Herman Melville; Ethel Merman; Rosie O'Donnell; Christopher Reeve; John D. Rockefeller; Norman Rockwell; Mickey Rooney; Eleanor Roosevelt; Franklin D. Roosevelt; Theodore Roosevelt; Jonas Salk; Barbra Streisand; Martin Van Buren; Mae West; Edith Wharton; and Walt Whitman.**

This goddess also appears on New York's state flag. On a dark blue field is the state's coat of arms. There, Liberty holds a pole topped with a Liberty cap, a symbol of freedom (its original name was the Phrygian cap; these were given to Roman slaves who had been liberated). At Liberty's feet lies a discarded crown, representing freedom from England at the end of the Revolutionary War. This symbol of an overthrown tyrant also appears on Virginia's flag; the liberty cap can be seen on the flags of several states.

To the right of Liberty is the goddess Justice. She is blindfolded to show that justice is blind against income, race, and religion. She carries the scales of justice to demonstrate how everyone should receive equal treatment under the law. Each goddess wears a string of pearls atop her head.

> Between 1990 and 2000, New York State's population increased by 5.5 percent to 18,976,457 people; 8,008,278, or nearly half of the state's citizens, live in New York City. The number rises to more than 21 million people when including the suburbs (the "Tri-State Area" includes New Jersey and Connecticut).

The coat of arms also includes a sun rising over the Hudson highlands and ships sailing on the Hudson River (a three-masted, square-rigged ship and a Hudson River sloop sail the river to signify commerce). It was Henry Hudson who first sailed up what would later be named the Hudson River. Above these images, an eagle rests on a globe, representing the Western Hemisphere, or the "New World."

New York's motto, *"Excelsior"* (meaning "Ever Higher" or "Ever Upward"), appears near the bottom of the flag, beneath the coat of arms. Scripted on a white ribbon, *"Excelsior"* is meant to express the idea of New Yorkers continuing to reach toward higher goals, including commerce and immigration as well as the arts, intellectual pursuits, and ecological conservation. New York's official fruit is the apple, and New York City's nickname is "The Big Apple." The state got its nickname in 1784 when George Washington took a tour. He was so impressed by the fertile land and beautiful waterways that he referred to New York as the "Seat of Empire," thus the "Empire State."

Nicknames
"Empire State"
"Vacationland"

Motto
"Ever Higher"

The image of the sun rising over the Hudson highlands harkens back to the time when New York first got its name. Originally called New Amsterdam by the Dutch, this land, with its important harbor and its majestic river, its vast farmlands, and its potential for industry, was acquired by the British in 1664. They promptly named the colony New York after the Duke of York.

On July 26, 1788, representatives from the state legislature signed the United States Constitution. In that same year, they adopted the state's first official flag (the original can be found at The Albany Institute of History and Art). Almost one hundred years later, Lady Liberty would assume her post beneath the southern tip of Manhattan. And in 1901, state representatives discarded the state's first flag and adopted a variation of a Revolutionary War flag as the state's official flag. On a tragic day one hundred years after this legislation was passed, New York would be confronted with its greatest challenge as terrorists attacked the World Trade Center. The Statue of Liberty survived and still stands proudly on Liberty Island and the flag of New York State still waves along with the American flag.

> **Niagara Falls is not the state's highest waterfall. This honor goes to Taughannock Falls, in Ulysses. At 215 feet, it is the highest waterfall east of the Rockies.**

> **Uncle Sam was actually a meatpacker from the small city of Troy. During the War of 1812, Sam Wilson stamped "U.S. Beef" on his meat and soldiers interpreted this as Uncle Sam's Beef! His image, costumed in patriotic garb, was later used to represent the United States.**

North Carolina

Admitted

November 21, 1789

Sixty years after separating from South Carolina to form its own colony, North Carolina was granted statehood. This made North Carolina the twelfth state to sign the United States Constitution and join the Union. Although North Carolina attained statehood on November 21, 1789, it would not adopt an official flag until March 9, 1865. Since then there has been no change to the state flag.

It was in 1861, at the legislative meeting to decide whether or not to secede, that the idea of a North Carolina flag was presented. As in other southern states, talk of secession and war inspired legislators to commission a state flag. Ironically, North Carolina's original design featured the red, white, and blue of the American flag. It also included two dates: "May 20, 1775," for the Mecklenburg Declaration of Independence (the citizens of Mecklenburg County, according to local folklore, proclaimed their independence from the British before anyone else in the colonies), and "May 20, 1861," for the day North Carolina seceded from the Union.

> The state motto, *"Esse Quam Videri,"* means "To be rather than to seem." Alluding to integrity and genuineness, *"Esse Quam Videri"* has been used in North Carolina since the General Assembly adopted it in 1893.

Once the war ended, the design of North Carolina's state flag was altered for the first and only time. In a simple move of reconciliation and patriotism, the date of secession was removed. The date of the Mecklenburg Declaration of Independence remained, and the date of the Halifax Resolves, "April 12, 1776," was added. This was in appreciation of the aggressive role that North Carolina played during the American Revolutionary War. Samuel Johnston, a future governor and congressman for North Carolina, had overseen the Halifax Resolves, a declaration of independence for the colonies. There were eighty-three delegates present in Halifax for the Fourth Provincial Congress. They voted unanimously to adopt the Halifax Resolves, which stated, among other things, that the leaders of the colonies would meet to establish independence and to determine rules—essentially, to organize themselves as a nation. Although the thirteen colonies were referred to as the "United Colonies" in this document, they would soon thereafter be known as the thirteen states—the United States.

On the state flag, the dates of the Mecklenburg Declaration of Independence and Halifax Resolves appear on a field of blue that runs vertically along the hoist side of the flag (closest to the staff or flagpole). This field is sometimes referred to as the "union" of the flag. The dates appear in a golden arc, above and below a large white star and the gold initials "N" and "C." This broad band of color occupies one-third of the flag. The remaining two-thirds of the flag are described as follows in a state statute: "The fly of the flag shall consist of two equally proportioned bars; the upper bar to be red, the lower bar to be white." The statute also states that the width of the flag should be two-thirds of the length.

On November 21, 1789, North Carolina, once again under the guidance of Samuel Johnston, finally ratified the United States Constitution. Representatives were pleased to see that the Bill of Rights had been added; it was out of concern for individual rights, including states' rights, that they had first rejected the Constitution. In 1865, North Carolina officially adopted its state flag, and three years later, the state was accepted back into the Union.

Unlike Georgia and Mississippi, North Carolina has avoided controversy over their red, white, and blue flag. This is because every morning, flags that do not offend any of the citizens are raised all across this twelfth state.

> **North Carolina's first nickname was the "Old North State,"** referring to the split from South Carolina in 1729. Whereas people in the sister state to the south were farming rice and indigo, Old North Staters were making money from tar, pitch, and turpentine. This, combined with a legend that troops from North Carolina stuck to their guns during battle, led to another nickname: the "Tar Heel State." When General Robert E. Lee complimented the state's troops for refusing to retreat (as if they had tar on their heels, holding them in their place), he said, "God bless the Tar Heel boys." And thus, a new nickname was born.

Another aspect of life in North Carolina that lends to the idea of America as a melting pot is the rapidly growing, and changing, population. From 1990 to 2000, the population of North Carolina increased by more than one million people. People of all

> **The University of North Carolina was the first public university in the United States.**

races and cultures have chosen to pursue the American dream in North Carolina. While almost two-thirds of the state's population is white, nearly one-third is African-American. The state is also home to a significant number of Native Americans (North Carolina's Cherokee are the dominant tribe, having managed to avoid the "Trail of Tears" Indian Removal program of the early 1800s), Hispanics, and Asians. Thinking back to the Mecklenburg Declaration and the Halifax Resolves, North Carolinians today know that these important dates belong on their state flag. It was in 1775 and 1776 that their forefathers took the first steps toward the dream of independence for all.

> **Since New Hampshire and North Carolina are separated by almost one thousand miles, you might think that they have nothing in common. Not so. Granite is the official state rock for both states. Just as there are granite mountains and granite quarries up north, there are quarries and mountains down south.**

Rhode Island

Rhode Island

Admitted

May 29, 1790

There are two possible origins of the name Rhode Island. One has been embraced by the state's government while the other is more folklore than fact. Some say that in 1614, Dutch explorer Adriaen Block's first impression of the land was the red clay lining the shores of Narragansett Bay. The name he gave to this coastal area was *Roodt Eylandt*, which is Dutch for "red island." In turn, when the British took control of the colony, they anglicized the name, changing it to "Rhode Island." The second theory, as seen on Rhode Island's official website, gives credit to Italian explorer Giovanni da Verazzano. Verazzano compared the island that would someday be known as Block Island to the Mediterranean Isle of Rhodes as he sailed towards Narragansett Bay in 1524. One credit that can be given to Block with absolute certainty is Block Island. He had ego enough to name the handsome island after himself!

> **Rhode Island is home to the oldest schoolhouse in the United States of America. The building was erected in Portsmouth in 1716.**

Rhode Islanders take pride in the claim that theirs was the first colony to declare its independence from Great Britain. This took place on May 4, 1776. One hundred and twenty-one years later, the Rhode Island General Assembly adopted the state's current flag.

On the flag, a golden anchor speaks to the state's extensive coastline, while thirteen golden stars confirm Rhode Island's historical place among the origi-

> **The official name of Rhode Island, "State of Rhode Island and Providence Plantations," stands in direct contrast to the state's size. At 1,214 square miles, Rhode Island is easily America's smallest state. Delaware is the second-smallest and has twice as much land as Rhode Island!**
>
> **"Little Rhody" is, fittingly enough, one of the state's nicknames. It is only thirty-seven miles long and forty-eight miles wide, but has almost four hundred miles of coastline. This explains its other nickname: the "Ocean State."**

nal thirteen colonies. Although New Hampshire was the ninth state to ratify the United States Constitution, thereby establishing that document as the framework for our government, it was still important to the federal government that the rest of the colonies—Virginia, New York, North Carolina, and Rhode Island—give their approval. When Rhode Island's General Assembly voted on May 29, 1790, to ratify, all thirteen original colonies were on board. The first thirteen states were truly united.

Nevertheless, Rhode Island's vote was extremely close; if just two votes had been cast differently, the Constitution would not have been accepted. Thirty-four representatives voted in favor of joining the Union while thirty-two voted against—not an overwhelming show of support for the United States. Fiercely independent, many Rhode Islanders were wary of suffering under the same monarchical constraints experienced under Great Britain's King George III. Most citizens did not know what, exactly, a president would have the power to do. George Washington himself is said to have been unsure about what was expected of him as the nation's first president, so who could blame the citizens for their concern? But in Rhode Island enough of the people were optimistic; they had hope, and the vote passed.

> **The portrait of George Washington found on the United States $1 bill was painted by Rhode Islander Gilbert Stuart. This portrait would eventually grace the flag of the state of Washington.**

Rhode Island's General Assembly adopted the official state flag in its January 1897 session. Only two other states, New York and New Jersey, had bothered to adopt an official "banner" by this time. The golden anchor, certainly the most distinct symbol on the flag, harkens back to 1647 when the Providence Plantations were established, and the colony chose the anchor as its seal. The anchor was a common symbol at this time because people depended so much on the seas for travel and the transport of goods. The word "Hope" was also added to the state seal at this time.

Rhode Island's modern flag consists of a white field featuring "Hope" in gold on a banner of blue. The thirteen stars are gold, as are the anchor and the flag's three fringe edges. Unlike with most state flags, these images appear

All summer long, concerts are held at Newport's Fort Adams State Park. Perhaps the most famous of them all is the Newport Folk Festival, which recently celebrated its fortieth anniversary. The Newport Jazz Festival, founded in 1954, had met with such success that the promoters decided to host a second music festival and launched the Folk Festival in 1959. Jazz pianist George Wein was the creative genius behind both events.

on both sides of the Rhode Island flag. "Hope" not only appears on the flag, it is the state's official motto.

Rhode Island was founded by Puritan minister Roger Williams, who came to the New World in the hopes of finding religious freedom. Williams arrived in Boston in 1631. Massachusetts, however, did not offer enough of the freedom that Williams sought; for example, the government there did not yet honor the separation of church and state. So Williams moved south and established a settlement in Rhode Island. Thankful for his good fortune in finding such a place to live, he named this new town Providence. To this day, Providence serves as the capital of Rhode Island, and Williams is considered to be the father of the state.

Williams founded the first Baptist church in the United States. It is no wonder then that the word *"Hope"* appears on the flag. Williams had such high hopes for the New World, and in the continuing debate over separation of church and state, a debate in which the "separatists" are still winning, he would not be disappointed.

Vermont

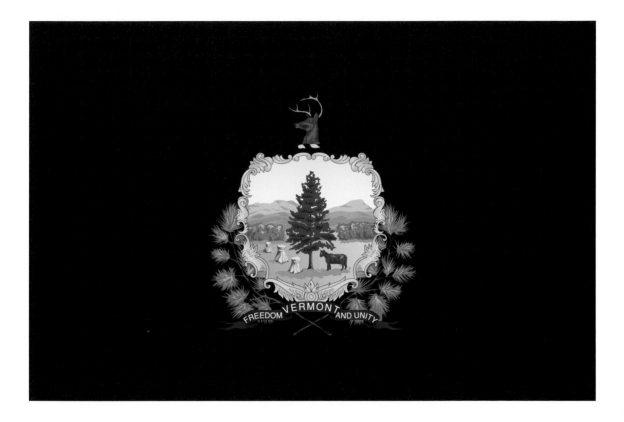

53

I n 1777, Vermont declared itself an independent republic. For fourteen years, this "nation" was able to maintain its freedom. One of the tenets of Vermont was to ban slavery in its constitution, long before this issue was ever addressed in the Constitution of the United States. On March 4, 1791, Vermont finally agreed, under pressure from the U.S. Congress, to become a part of the United States. Some modern-day residents, however, still want to return to that state of independence.

Vermont was the first state to join the Union that was not one of the original thirteen colonies. One year later Kentucky became the fifteenth state. Just as the country was changing so, too, was its flag. By a 1794 Act of Congress, the United States flag would now feature fifteen stars for fifteen states. This design remained unchanged until 1818 and was the flag that inspired Francis Scott Key to write "The Star Spangled Banner" during the War of 1812. The fifteen-star flag is sometimes referred to as the Fort McHenry Flag, because Key was watching the attack on Maryland's Fort McHenry when he wrote his poem. One of these Fort McHenry Flags is still held by the Vermont Historical Society.

Before adopting its current flag, Vermont employed several state flags, all of which had been flown by its regiments during the Civil War, the Spanish-American War, and World War I. The only flaw of these earlier versions was that they looked very much like the American flag; the state that had fought for so long to maintain independence had chosen to use red and white stripes on their state flag! It was virtually impossible to tell the Vermont flag from the

During the Revolutionary War, Ethan Allen and his Green Mountain Boys led an attack on Fort Ticonderoga and captured it from Great Britain. Before the war ended, the British would try to negotiate with Allen. They wanted to make Vermont a part of Canada. You can guess what his answer was.

The first "Stars and Stripes" flag ever flown was carried by the Green Mountain Boys at the Revolutionary War Battle of Bennington on August 16, 1777. This flag can still be seen at the Bennington Historical Museum.

American flag when hanging limp on a windless day, and Vermont's legislators decided it was time to distinguish their flag. In 1919, they adopted a new design.

"Verd Mont" is French for "Green Mountain," and the state's mountains do appear on its flag. On a field of blue is the state coat of arms, a picturesque representation of Vermont's natural beauty. At the center is a pine tree set against green fields and, in the background, the Green Mountains. It is generally accepted that these two mountains are Camel's Hump and Mt. Mansfield, as seen from Burlington. This view was selected because it is most likely what Samuel de Champlain saw when he first sailed up Lake Champlain. Champlain is credited as being the first European explorer to sail this lake.

Above this scene is a stag's head, facing west. To the right of the pine tree stands a red cow; to the left, three sheaves of wheat. Vermont may be known for its tourism (out-of-state visitors are referred to as "Flatlanders"), but agriculture has always been an important means of income for Vermonters. Pine boughs border the seal on the left and right. Crossing the boughs is a crimson banner bearing the name "Vermont" and the state motto, "Freedom and Unity." "Freedom" appears to the left of the state name, while "Unity" appears to the right. One has to wonder if this was done purposely, to show that state residents value their freedom more than a sense of unity with the rest of the country.

The independent thinking in Vermont was evident in 1858, when all African Americans who had been brought into the state were freed. This was in direct contrast to federal law. Then, in 1940, Vermont's state legislature declared war on Germany before the United States could even do so! And today

Montpelier may be the state capital, but Burlington is Vermont's largest city. In keeping with Vermont's diminutive size, Burlington's population, according to the 2000 census, was only 39,127. Every September, though, the population of the city increases significantly as thousands of students return to the University of Vermont for another year of studies.

Motto
"Freedom and Unity"

some citizens are still calling for secession and a return to that earlier independence. Members of the Vermont Republican Army and the Vermont Sovereignty Project (VTSP) feel that the federal government has too much control over the states and that no democracy can be properly run on such a grand scale. Contrary to what some Flatlanders might believe, the VTSP clearly states on its Website that new members must promise to act peacefully when sworn in. This is not a militia group; this a group that takes to heart the Tenth Amendment ("The powers not delegated to the United States by the Constitution, nor prohibited by it to the States, are reserved to the States respectively, or to the people"). They are interpreting the United States Constitution in a literal manner (meaning that the Constitution is not open to interpretation; this is also called "strict construction").

> **Vermont's state constitution was the first in the nation to abolish the requirement that voters must be property owners.**

Secessionists represent only a small portion of Vermonters. However, it is a movement worth paying attention to given that secession has played such an intriguing role in our nation's history. The situation in modern day Vermont is reminiscent of the first years of the United States Constitution, when so many states were hesitant to give up their hard-fought freedom to the federal government.

Vermont may be our fifth-smallest state, and the second-smallest in population (613,090 citizens according to the 2000 census), but this state represents two of the best things about our nation: natural beauty and a passion for freedom.

Kentucky

Kentucky

Admitted

June 1, 1792

T he state flag of Kentucky is a simple depiction of a pioneer and a statesman shaking hands on a field of blue. Both figures could very well have been modeled after the frontiersman Daniel Boone, who explored Kentucky and established settlements like Boonseboro, as well as representing his friends and neighbors in the Virginia legislature.

Kentucky was originally established, in 1776, as a county in western Virginia. Although men from Kentucky fought in the American Revolutionary War, they did not do so under a Kentucky flag. Statehood was still sixteen years away for them.

In 1792, the Commonwealth of Kentucky was admitted to the Union, the fifteenth state to be granted statehood and the first west of the Appalachian Mountains. Some residents of the state, though, did not see entering the Union as an honor or a necessity. Although Kentucky never claimed to be its own nation, certain citizens, like those in Vermont, wanted to maintain their independence from the United States. In particular, they saw how the Spanish could make for profitable trading partners located, as they were, just down the Mississippi in New Orleans. The hope was that by being a part of Spain's territorial holdings, Kentucky's economy would receive a real boost. General James Wilkinson even took an oath of allegiance with the Spanish; luckily, statehood came before any further steps could be taken to put his plan into effect.

The image of the two forefathers on the Kentucky flag comes from the state seal. The pioneer and the statesman symbolize both sides of early life in Kentucky and are also meant to represent the state's motto, "United We Stand, Divided We Fall." The motto appears within the state seal, encircling

> Although Kentucky is famous for its coal mines, the state has other sources of manufacturing income. Thus, Kentuckians have one state emblem that is unlike any other state's. According to House Bill 123, signed into legislation in 2000, "The mag wheel is named and designated as the official hubcap of Kentucky." This follows an existing clause: "WHEREAS, Kentucky is a state which shows its pride by the quality of its hubcaps."

the two men. This phrase gained national prominence during the Civil War. Goldenrod, the state flower, forms a half circle around the bottom of the seal. Above the pioneer and the statesman are the words "Commonwealth of Kentucky." The General Assembly authorized an official state seal for Kentucky in 1792.

In 1918, the General Assembly adopted the state's first official flag, but could not agree on the final specifications for ten years. Finally, in 1928, these legislators were satisfied and gave their approval to the state flag. All of the flag's specifications, including size, color and even the material it can be embroidered on, are described in Kentucky state statute. Although the actual size does not matter, "the length shall be one and nine-tenths times the width and the diameter of the seal and encirclement shall be approximately two-thirds the width of the flag." The state statute was altered regarding the exact specifications of the flag in 1962, but the appearance of the flag has remained the same ever since 1918.

Kentucky played an interesting role in the Civil War. Not only was it a border state between the North and South, it also provided an important route for transporting troops and supplies. Before the war, in

> **Kentucky is growing rapidly. According to the 2000 census, the state's population was 4,041,769 people, a ten percent increase over 1990's population.**

1833, the Kentucky state legislature had outlawed slavery. The state's economy relied on small farms (tobacco, soybeans, and corn, for example) rather than large plantations (cotton is not farmed in Kentucky), so slaves were not a necessity. In 1850 the General Assembly made slave trading and slave ownership legal again, but when the Civil War began, Kentucky tried to remain neutral. The Confederacy sealed its own fate with Kentucky, however, when Confederate soldiers set up camp in the south of Kentucky. The state's people quickly grew upset and the General Assembly knew that they would have to take action. They had just determined that they would go to battle with the intruding Rebels when General Ulysses S. Grant (who would go on to be the eighteenth president of the U.S.) did the work for them. His troops chased the Confederates southward, freeing Kentucky from their encampments, and

Nickname
"Bluegrass State"

Motto
"United We Stand, Divided We Fall"

In 1999, the United States Mint began its "50 State Quarter" program. The quarters are being released in the order in which the states joined the Union. Kentucky's quarter, the fifteenth in the series, was released on October 18, 2001. Each state quarter features a unique design. Kentucky's shows the Federal Hill mansion, built by local judge John Rowan and known throughout the state as "My Old Kentucky Home." A thoroughbred racehorse also appears on the coin, standing behind a fence, in reference to the nation's oldest annual horse race, the Kentucky Derby.

neutrality was no longer a possibility. Kentucky was with the Union. Sadly, though, men from the state ended up fighting for both the North and the South. It truly was a war of neighbor versus neighbor and brother versus brother in Kentucky.

While goldenrod is featured on the state flag, Kentucky is known as the "Bluegrass State." There are many varieties of bluegrass; all are perennial and most have bluish green foliage, thus the name. The best known of all the bluegrasses is Kentucky Bluegrass, and a large area of land in the northern part of the state is known as the Bluegrass Region. This large expanse of land attracted the majority of the pioneers when they first began to settle Kentucky. Louisville, Lexington, and the state's capital, Frankfort, are all found in the Bluegrass Region. It was in Frankfort that the pioneer first embraced the statesman as Kentucky became America's fifteenth state.

Tennessee

From 1787 to 1792, fifteen states became a part of the United States. The first was Delaware; the last was Kentucky. Then, for four years the size of the country remained stable, until Tennessee joined the Union in 1796.

In the years following the Revolutionary War, the people of eastern Tennessee claimed state status; they named their state Frankland and later, Franklin. This frontier land had once been a part of North Carolina, but in 1784 North Carolina ceded its claim to the federal government. Angry at not having any input in this decision and worried about protecting themselves against Native American attack, residents decided to form their own government. They elected John Sevier, a hero from the Revolutionary War, governor. This temporary and unofficial (they never received Congressional recognition) statehood lasted for four years, from 1784 to 1788, until North Carolina took control again. But when North Carolina was granted statehood, in 1789, eastern Tennessee was not included within its boundaries. Instead, the federal government named the area the Southwest Territory.

It was on June 21, 1796, that Tennessee became the sixteenth state to join the Union. This meant that Tennessee *was* the official frontier of the United States of America. The western edge of the state, and of the country, was marked by the mighty Mississippi River. Soon, statehood would come to the lands west of the Mississippi as America continued to grow.

It would take more than a hundred years for Tennessee to adopt a state flag. LeRoy Reeves, a soldier from the Third Regiment of the Tennessee Infantry, designed the flag in the late 1890s. It is a simple but bold design of

Memphis is Tennessee's largest city, but Nashville is the state's most beloved city. Not only is it the state capital, Nashville has long been seen as *the* mecca of country music. It is a major recording center and home to the Grand Ol' Opry.

Nashville is sometimes referred to as the "Athens of the South," because so many of its buildings are of a classical design. Nashville is also home to many colleges and universities, including Vanderbilt University.

three stars in a blue circle, set against a red field. Reeves described his flag as follows: "The three stars are of pure white, representing the three grand divisions of the state." These divisions are East Tennessee, which is best known for the Great Smoky Mountains, Middle Tennessee, which is home to the Tennessee River and is known as "bluegrass country," and West Tennessee, which lies between the Tennessee and Mississippi Rivers and is cotton country. Reeves continued, "They are bound together by the endless circle of the blue field. The symbol being three bound together in one—an indissoluble trinity. The large field is crimson. The final blue bar relieves the sameness of the crimson field and prevents the flag from showing too much crimson when hanging limp. The white edgings contrast more strongly the other colors." This description can be found in Tennessee's *Blue Book*.

The flag of Tennessee might not be in the top ten of the "Great NAVA Survey of 2001" (it was ranked fourteenth out of seventy-two flags), but Reeves's design has certainly accomplished color, simplicity, distinctness, and symbolism. For example, Reeves showed foresight and the vision, vexillologically speaking, when he suggested the band of blue to provide variety of color.

Tennessee is known for its natural beauty and resources. The state features twenty-three state parks that cover almost 132,000 acres. The Great Smoky Mountains National Park, Cherokee National Forest, and Cumberland Gap National Historical Park are three of the state's most popular parks.

Nicknames

"Big Bend State"
"Volunteer State"

Motto

"Agriculture and Commerce"

The Tennessee Legislature adopted this distinctive flag on April 17, 1905. Although Reeves's description paints a complete picture, the legislators were compelled to pass Chapter 498 of the Public Acts of 1905 in order to describe the flag in greater detail. The colors of the state flag have an extra appeal for Tennessee's legislators and citizens: they are the same red, white, and blue as seen on the American flag.

Residents of the state are called Tennesseans. Since 1990, the number of Tennesseans has increased drastically. The state experienced a 16.7 percent increase in population, according to the 2000 census. Memphis, Chattanooga, Knoxville, and Nashville have experienced the most growth. Tennesseans are also called Volunteers or Benders; both are references to state nicknames. The "Big Bend State" refers to the way the Tennessee River flows into Alabama and then curls back up into western Tennessee as it makes its way to the Ohio River. The most commonly used nickname for Tennessee, though, is the "Volunteer State," a name it earned during the War of 1812, when soldiers from Tennessee fought courageously against the British in the Battle of New Orleans. They did so under fellow Tennessean, General Andrew Jackson.

Andrew Jackson is one of the most famous Tennesseans. He went on to become the seventh president of the United States and was in office from 1829 to 1837. Another famous Tennessean, who served under General Jackson, was Davy Crockett. Known primarily as a frontiersman, Crockett was elected to the state legislature and then to the United States Congress. After he began to oppose President Jackson's Indian Removal policies, he was pegged as a conservative and lost his bid for reelection in 1835. Returning to the battlefield, Crockett lost his life defending the Alamo.

> **The Tennessee Department of Health keeps track of a variety of statistics. For example, on its website you'll find the top twenty-five first names of children born in Tennessee in 2001. The number-one name for girls was Hannah, followed by Madison and Emily. Jacob, William, and Joshua were the top three boys' names.**

Ohio

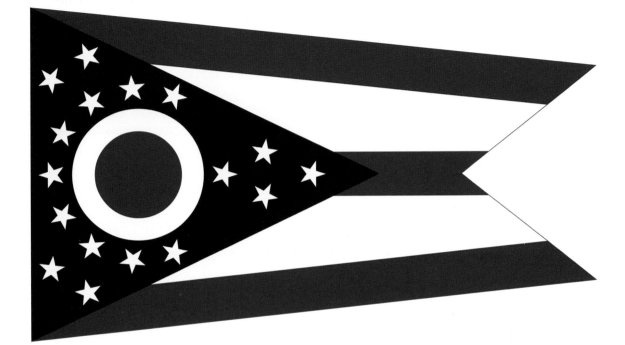

65

Ohio

Admitted

March 1, 1803

If you looked at the cover of this book before starting to read, one flag probably stood out. Only one of fifty state flags is *not* a rectangle. Only one can lay claim to being totally different in shape and design from all the rest. This flag belongs to Ohio.

Ohio's flag is best described as a pennant. Most often seen on ships or at yacht clubs, the shape of this flag is referred to by vexillologists as a pennant with a swallowtail tip. This particular design is also referred to now as the Ohio burgee (burgee is another term for swallowtail). This innovative flag was designed by John Eisemann, an architect, and was adopted by the state's General Assembly in 1902.

The "O" in the center of the blue field is doubly symbolic. The first reference is obvious: "O" is for Ohio. It is also an artistic representation of a buckeye and a reference to the state nickname, the "Buckeye State." Buckeyes are the nuts that fall from the many buckeye trees found in Ohio. They are round and, according to the Native Americans who named them, looked like a buck's eye. William Henry Harrison was born in Virginia, but settled in Ohio after defeating the Native Americans at the Battle of Tippecanoe. When Harrison ran for president, his critics said that he was better suited for sitting in a log cabin than the White House. His supporters decided to embrace this back woods image and started to carry buckeye canes. When Harrison beat the incumbent, Martin Van Buren, the buckeye became associated with Ohio.

The flag's blue field is located near the staff, or flagpole. Within this field is the "O" surrounded by thirteen white stars, for the thirteen original states.

> **According to the 2000 census, Ohio's population is 11,353,140. This makes it the seventh-most-populous state in the United States. A state's population determines its number of representatives to Congress and number of electoral votes; Ohio sends nineteen representatives to Washington, D.C., to serve in Congress. During the 2000 election, Ohio had twenty-one electoral votes. George W. Bush received fifty percent of the state's popular votes, which means that all twenty-one electoral votes were cast in his favor.**

The blue field is an isoceles triangle and there are four additional stars in the field's rightmost peak, distanced enough from the other stars to show the proper respect. These stars represent Vermont, Kentucky, Tennessee, and Ohio, the four states that joined the Union after the original thirteen.

Like several other state flags, Ohio's flag features the colors red, white, and blue. Three red stripes and two white stripes are located to the right of the blue triangular field and culminate in the two points of the swallowtail. The blue field is an acknowledgment of Ohio's hills and valleys, while the red and white stripes symbolize the state's roads and waterways.

These valleys and waterways have enabled Ohio to have more than just an agrarian economy. Railroads and highways crisscross the state, and Toledo and Cleveland are both port cities on Lake Erie, allowing for interstate commerce of manufactured goods. Finished products, such as steel and automobile parts, as well as raw materials such as coal, oil, iron and copper ore, also supplement Ohio's economy.

This land, with its subtle hills, Ohio River, and access to the Great Lakes, was granted to the United States by Great Britain as a part of the Treaty of Paris in 1783. Connecticut, Massachusetts, and Virginia all made claims to the land, and pioneers did not have an easy time establishing settlements as they battled with both Native Americans and the British troops who supported them. United States troops prevailed, and the land that would someday be Ohio was named the Northwest Territory in 1799.

Seven years had passed since the last state, Tennessee, was welcomed into the Union, but finally on March 1, 1803, America admitted its seventeenth state. North of Kentucky and south of Lake Erie, most of what had been referred to as the Northwest Territory would now be called Ohio.

Ohio gained statehood in 1803, so 2003 marks the two-hundredth anniversary, more commonly referred to as a bicentennial, of the "Buckeye State." The state's governor and General Assembly have granted a fifty-one-member Ohio Bicentennial Commission the authority to plan the state's year-long celebration. One highlight is the Bicentennial Barn Painting, which began in1998.

Virginia may be known as "The Mother of Presidents" (eight presidents were born there), but there are also eight presidents who can claim ties to Ohio. These are William Henry Harrison (ninth president, serving in 1841), Ulysses S. Grant (eighteenth president), Rutherford B. Hayes (nineteenth), James A. Garfield (twentieth, serving in 1881), Benjamin Harrison (twenty-third), William McKinley (twenty-fifth), William Howard Taft (twenty-seventh), and finally, Warren G. Harding (twenty-ninth). From Grant to Garfield, three presidents in a row hailed from Ohio. From 1869 to 1893 there were actually only eight years in which a man from Ohio was *not* the president of the United States of America!

Ironically, this name can be attributed to the people chased from the area by settlers. To the Iroquois, *Ohio* means "good river." The Ohio River, a tributary of the Mississippi River, drains into the Gulf of Mexico.

In addition to their waterways, Ohioans can be proud of their connection with flight. The state is home to twenty-four astronauts, including John Glenn and Neil Armstrong, the first people to walk on the moon. Orville Wright is also a native son of Ohio. Out of this has grown the state's unofficial motto, "The Birthplace of Aviation."

Louisiana

Admitted

April 30, 1812

In 1912, one hundred years after attaining state status, Louisiana's legislature adopted the current state flag. Although this same flag has been raised above the state every day ever since, the area that would someday become Louisiana has a long and varied history that includes many flags. In fact, it has flown more official flags, be they national or state flags, than any other state.

Louisiana's flag design is truly unique among all the state flags. Four eastern brown pelicans—a mother feeding three baby pelicans in the nest—are featured in the middle of a blue field. The eastern brown pelican is the state bird, and Louisiana is known as the "Pelican State." This name was passed down from the state's first settlers. Legend has it that these early Louisianans respected the area's indigenous pelicans because, when food was scarce, the birds would peck at their breasts until they bled in order to feed their young.

Hanging beneath the pelicans' nest is a white banner with the state motto lettered in blue: "Union, Justice, and Confidence."

As early as 1519, Spanish explorer Álonso Alvarez de Piñeda sailed along the shores of the Gulf of Mexico, discovering the mouth of the Mississippi River and flying the flag of Spain as he did. In 1682, the French explorer Sieur de La Salle claimed the land at the mouth of the Mississippi River for France. The French flag then flew over most of the land that La Salle had named Louisiana (for King Louis XIV of France) until Napoléon Bonaparte sold the region to the United States on April 30, 1803, as a part of the Louisiana Purchase. Before this transaction, some of the land was ceded to the British (in 1763, Great Britain gained land east of the Mississippi as a result of the French and Indian War), and some of the land continued to be controlled by the Spanish. In a secret treaty in 1762, France had given land to Spain; the colonists did not know about the change for almost two years. In 1800, the Spanish gave this land back to the French in another secret treaty. The Louisiana Purchase was only three years away. And after that important

> In 1986, Louisiana named an official state doughnut. It is the beignet, a French pastry, usually served with a dusting of powdered sugar. Fittingly enough, the official state drink is milk!

day in 1803, the American flag was the only national flag to ever fly over Louisiana again.

In 1810, colonists took control of an area that was situated in Spain's West Florida Territory. The land and its people would become a part of the Union soon enough. Louisiana is divided into parishes rather than counties, and the colonists in the Florida Parishes flew a flag known as the "Bonnie Blue." Although some stability would eventually come to the region, especially with statehood in 1812, Louisiana's flag would continue to evolve.

Louisiana, until now referred to as the Territory of Orleans, joined the Union on April 30, 1812. The United States was expanding westward and most historians see the $15 million Louisiana Purchase, completed exactly nine years before, as one of the defining moments in our nation's history. By 1812, the United States was eighteen states strong and twice as large as it had been before the Louisiana Purchase, but tumultuous times were coming; the issue of slavery had to be resolved, and it would take a war to do so.

At the onset of the Civil War, Louisiana actually spent two months as an unaffiliated state; in essence, it was an independent nation. On January 26, 1861, Louisiana seceded from the Union. Before joining the Confederacy, government officials flew a flag that featured a yellow star in a red field, buoyed by stripes of red, white, and blue. After Louisiana joined the Confederacy, it flew the "Stars and Bars," a flag that closely resembles the United States flag. Streaming away from the hoist side and a canton of blue were two broad red stripes and one broad white stripe. Seven white stars, placed in a circle, filled the field of blue. Then, from 1863 to 1865, Louisiana raised the Confederate Battle Flag. This is the flag that is most commonly associated with the Confederate States of America. There were seven stars for seven states on the first flag. The "Stars and Bars" was, after all, used to represent the original seven states (Louisiana, Mississippi, Florida, Alabama, Georgia, South Carolina, and Texas) of the Confederacy. By war's end, the Confederate States of America would consist of eleven states.

In 1865, the nation was reunited, and Louisiana experienced a long period of occupation by troops of the United States Army. This was called Reconstruction and was a time of healing for the country and of rebuilding in the South. When the federal government deemed a state ready, it would be

Nickname

"Pelican State"

Motto

"Union, Justice, and Confidence"

Louisiana has two official state songs: "You Are My Sunshine" and "Give Me Louisiana." "You Are My Sunshine," written by Jimmy H. Davis and Charles Mitchell, was recently featured in the film *O Brother, Where Art Thou?*

accepted back into the Union. It was actually the disputed presidential election of 1876 that freed Louisiana from the Reconstruction. In exchange for the withdrawal of troops, Louisiana gave its electoral votes to the Republicans so that Rutherford B. Hayes could win the election. Thus, in 1877 the longest period of occupation of any southern state came to an end.

Thirty-five years later, Louisiana would have a flag to fly beneath "Old Glory." The state adopted its pelican flag in 1912 and has yet to have reason to change it.

Indiana

In 1800, the United States government established the Indiana Territory. This territory included land that would later become Indiana, Illinois, and Wisconsin, as well as parts of Michigan and Minnesota. On December 11, 1816, Indiana ceased to be a part of the Indiana Territory, joining the Union as the nineteenth state. One hundred years after statehood, Indiana would adopt its first official state flag.

In 1916, Indiana celebrated its state centennial (one-hundredth anniversary). As a part of the celebration, the General Assembly called for a state flag contest. The Indiana Daughters of the American Revolution responded, organizing the contest and publicizing it throughout the state. An artist named Paul Hadley, from Mooresville, Indiana, submitted the winning design. The official description of the flag, taken from Indiana Code 1-2-2-1, is paraphrased as follows: The flag's dimensions will be three feet fly by two feet, or five feet fly by three feet, or any size that is in proportion to either of those dimensions. The field of the flag will be blue with nineteen stars and a flaming torch in buff (gold). Thirteen stars will be arranged in an outer circle, representing the original thirteen states; five stars will be arranged in a half circle below the torch and inside the outer circle of stars. These represent the states admitted to the Union prior to Indiana (Vermont, Kentucky, Tennessee, Ohio, and Louisiana) and after the original thirteen. The nineteenth star, slightly larger than the others and representing Indiana, will be placed above the flame of the torch. The outer circle of stars will be so arranged that one star appears directly in the middle at the top of the circle, and the word *Indiana* will be placed in a half

The Hoosiers of Indiana University are just one of the state's beloved basketball teams. Notre Dame, Purdue, Ball State, Butler, Valparaiso, and Evansville also have competitive basketball teams. Each has been invited to participate in the prestigious NCAA Division I basketball tournament. The Indiana Pacers are the state's National Basketball Association franchise while the Indiana Fever play in the Women's National Basketball Association. In 1986, the film *Hoosiers* captured the fervor that surrounds the sport in Indiana, even at the high school level.

circle above the star representing Indiana and midway between it and the star in the center above it. Rays will be shown radiating from the torch to the three stars on each side of the star in the upper center of the circle.

The centerpiece of Indiana's flag is the torch, representing enlightenment and liberty. The golden rays that extend outward stand for the far-reaching influence of these ideals.

The Indiana Territory was originally a part of the Northwest Territory. At first, this part of the country was a dangerous place for pioneers, but the United States Army soon cleared the way for settlement, forcing out the Native American residents in the process. General Anthony Wayne defeated a confederation of Native Americans at Fallen Timbers battlefield in 1794. The final blow for this regional confederation came when General William Henry Harrison (who would go on to be the ninth president of the United States) was victorious at the Battle of Tippecanoe, on Indiana's Tippecanoe River, in 1811. Despite this history, the Congress of the United States granted the nineteenth state the name *Indiana,* meaning "Land of Indians."

By 1816, when Indiana was granted statehood, more than 60,000 people had settled there. (A population of 60,000 is the minimal requirement for statehood.) Indiana is located midway between the South and Canada, and during the Civil War the Underground Railroad was present throughout the state. Although there was some proslavery sentiment there, presidential candidate Abraham Lincoln, who had spent his childhood in Indiana, won on the strength of Indiana's electoral votes in the election of 1860. Indiana did not secede, and the Underground Railroad was a foreshadowing of the state's future motto: "The Crossroads of America." Today, many interstate highways and train lines pass through the state, bridging the East and the West.

The state nickname is the "Hoosier State," and residents are called Hoosiers. While the origin of this nickname is unknown, there are several theories. The most commonly accepted comes from Jacob Piatt Dunn, Jr., an

Indiana historian. The name "Hoosier" was used in the early-nineteenth-century South to describe woodsmen or people who lived in the hills. Immigrants from Cumberland, England—where the word *hoo* means "hill"—first settled in the hills of Tennessee and West Virginia. Their descendants eventually migrated to the hills of southern Indiana. Some other fun but unconfirmed theories include anecdotes of early Hoosiers answering the door by yelling "Who's yere?" as well as Hoosiers being such tough fighters that they used to bite off the ears of their enemies ("Whose ear?")!

In 1820, eight stars were added to the official flag of the United States. The flag had featured fifteen stars since 1814, but so many states were being added to the Union, Indiana included, that the United States flag had to be updated. There were now twenty-three stars on the flag, along with thirteen stripes to represent the thirteen original colonies.

> **The Mound Builders were Indiana's earliest known inhabitants. Their mysterious mounds have been found in states from the Great Lakes to the Gulf of Mexico. Between 500 B.C. and 1000 A.D., these Native Americans built their mounds, some of which stand up to sixty-five feet tall and measure up to one hundred twenty acres. Although the mounds served several purposes, it is believed that they were often used as crypts, much like the pyramids in Egypt, to house the dead of important families.**

Mississippi

On December 10, 1817, statehood was granted to Mississippi, and the United States welcomed its twentieth state into the Union. The first Mississippi state flag was adopted in 1861, but it was not until February 7, 1894, that a committee appointed by state legislators would adopt the current state flag. This flag would survive controversy and still flies overhead today.

The flag committee chose a design that featured a "union square" in the upper left canton, or corner, of the flag. The field of this canton included a red background with a blue saltire (or Greek cross) that contains thirteen five-pointed white stars (also referred to as mullets). This saltire and its stars, so often associated with the Rebels of the South and the Confederate Battle Flag, are not, as some would believe, a tribute to the Confederate states. There were only eleven Confederate states; these stars actually represent the original thirteen states. Next to the union square, the national colors of red, white, and blue stretch to the hoist.

When Mississippi seceded from the Union in 1861, it did so as a sovereign nation. During this time, the state flew the flag that had served as its unofficial flag since that December day when Mississippi became the twentieth state. This simple design, a white star on a blue field, was known as the "Bonnie Blue" flag. (Louisiana also flew a "Bonnie Blue" flag.) But with the sectionalism that came during the years leading up to the Civil War, many states made adopting an official flag a priority. On January 26, 1861, the Mississippi secession convention decided not only to break ties with the Union, but also to adopt a totally new flag. The "Magnolia Flag" featured the "Bonnie Blue" design in the upper left canton as well as a magnolia tree and a band of red along the hoist. This was Mississippi's first official state flag, and it flew above the state's troops throughout the Civil War.

The origin of one our most popular toys is credited to an incident involving President Teddy Roosevelt. While hunting in Mississippi, he refused to shoot a bear cub because there was no sport in it. The story spread and Morris Michtom, a New York entrepreneur, created the first Teddy Bear.

The state's second flag, adopted in 1894, would be one of the most controversial flags the country has ever known. At the root of this controversy was the inclusion of the Confederate Battle Flag in the canton of this new state flag. Mississippi is now the only state in the Union to feature this flag so prominently, although Georgia does incorporate a smaller version of its former flag (including the Confederate Battle Flag) in its new state flag.

In response to several proposals and protests, Mississippi Governor Ronnie Musgrove agreed to House Bill 524. The bill, signed on January 12, 2001, called for Mississippi's Secretary of State to organize a vote; the people of Mississippi would decide the fate of their state flag. Two flags appeared on the ballot: the existing flag and an alternate, which has a similar appearance except that the canton is a blue field with a circular pattern of twenty white stars. The twentieth star, centered among the other stars, is slightly larger than the others and represents Mississippi. Absentee balloting was allowed, but write-in votes were not. This way the choice was simple: one or the other; the traditional or the new.

Even if voters had chosen the alternate flag, none of the existing memorials and monuments in Mississippi would have been altered. The government planned to be very careful about preserving the past while moving toward the future. But despite all the years of complaint and controversy, this move would not be necessary. On April 17, 2001, Mississippians voted overwhelmingly, sixty-five percent to thirty-five percent, in favor of their one-hundred-seven-year-old flag. It is certainly the hope of that sixty-five percent that this vote will put the issue to rest.

Although the flag is important to Mississippi's people, the state's most enduring symbol is its mighty river. The name *Mississippi* came from the river,

> Mississippi's state mammal is the bottlenose dolphin. With the Mississippi Sound, and access to the Gulf of Mexico, Mississippi actually does have a coastline that attracts these animals. Bottlenose dolphins are whales with tiny blowholes (they need to breathe but can hold their breath for several minutes) and sharp teeth. They can grow to be up to twenty-five feet long.

and the river's name came from the local Native Americans. To the Ojibwa tribe, *mici zibi* means "long river" or "great river." European arrivals anglicized the Ojibwa's words to *Mississippi*. Cotton is still Mississippi's number-one crop, and farms occupy almost half of the state's land. In particular, the fertile soil of the Yazoo-Mississippi delta allows farmers to grow cotton as well as soybeans and rice.

The state motto, *"Virtute et armis"* (meaning "By valor and arms"), speaks to the history of Mississippi and may in part explain why it is so important to so many of the state's residents to keep that history alive. To these people, recognizing those who fought valiantly for the state, for the United States, and for the Confederacy is as important as remembering what Mississippians refer to as the "Old South." For them, the flag offers this reminder. Residents state that slavery is not a part of this heritage—at least not the part they care to celebrate. It is a difficult, and often painful, matter to decide. But in 2001, the voters of Mississippi made clear how they felt. Like it or not, democracy was the deciding factor.

> **Mississippi is the birthplace of many of America's most beloved and talented writers. The following is a list of these authors and their most memorable works: Jimmy Buffett *(Tales from Margaritaville)*, William Faulkner *(The Sound and the Fury)*, Richard Ford *(The Sportswriter)*, John Grisham *(The Firm)*, Thomas Harris *(The Silence of the Lambs)*, Eudora Welty *(The Optimist's Daughter)*, Tennessee Williams *(Cat on a Hot Tin Roof)*, Richard Wright *(Native Son)*, and Willie Morris *(North Toward Home)*.**

Illinois

For six years starting in 1816, the United States added one state every year. The sequence began with Indiana and ended with Missouri. This period was also the beginning of the free state versus slave state debate.

It was in the middle of this state-a-year streak, on December 3, 1818, that Illinois became the twenty-first state in the Union. The state adopted its official flag almost one hundred years later, in 1915. The flag's design is actually the state seal with the name of the state in bold capital script below. But the state's name did not always appear on the flag.

The addition of "Illinois" came at the request of a soldier who was stationed in Vietnam. Chief Petty Officer Bruce McDaniel, from Waverly, Illinois, wrote to his state's General Assembly and pointed out that Illinois's flag lacked an identifying mark or moniker. Whenever he looked around the mess hall, he could not distinguish his flag from many of the other flags. In turn, anyone who could not recognize the state seal of Illinois would not know whose flag it was. His argument was convincing, and in 1969 the General Assembly demonstrated its agreement by adding "Illinois" to the flag. It is fitting that one of the state's residents was able to implement this change; after all, it was the people of Illinois who campaigned for a state flag in the first place.

As was the case in several states, this campaign began with the Daughters of the American Revolution. They held a state flag contest and offered a $25

> How can a state located in the middle of a continent have port cities? And why do people from Illinois consider their state to be a "crossroad" state? One of Illinois's borders runs along Lake Michigan. Chicago, the state's largest city, is located on this Great Lake as well. Several rivers, including the Illinois, the Mississippi, the Ohio, and the Wabash, also help make Illinois a center of commerce and trade, and the Mississippi links the state to the Gulf of Mexico. In addition, Chicago's O'Hare International Airport has earned the title "Nation's Busiest Airport" several times.

prize for the best design. Thirty-five submissions were received, and a panel of judges chose Lucy Derwent's flag. The Daughters of the American Revolution then presented the design to the General Assembly, which signed it into law on July 16, 1915. Fifty-four years later, Officer McDaniel's addition was agreed upon. Other than that, the flag has gone unchanged since its adoption.

The flag is a field of white with the state seal in the center. The seal is an impressively patriotic portrait: a bald eagle stands upon a rock on a prairie field, the sun emitting glorious rays in the background. Hanging from the bald eagle's beak is a banner reading "State Sovereignty, National Union," the official state motto and a reference to Illinois's independence from, and coexistence with, the United States government. Federalism was a crucial concept for the states that first agreed to join the Union. British soldiers had been on American soil just four years before Illinois was granted statehood, and citizens wanted to make sure that the federal government did not hold too much power. They did not want their president to be the equivalent of a monarch. Autonomy and cooperation are the themes of Illinois's motto.

There are two dates on the bald eagle's perch: "1818," the year Illinois became a state, and "1868," the year the state seal became official. Just as the bald eagle is a patriotic symbol, so too is the shield the bird holds in its talons. Illinois's General Assembly acknowledged the original colonies-turned-states; thirteen stars and thirteen stripes decorate the shield.

The state seal has not escaped controversy, and its story has become a bit of local folklore. During the Civil War, Illinois Secretary of State Sharon Tyndale wanted to change the order of the wording on the banner to read "National Union, State Sovereignty." Upset about the secession of southern states, Tyndale wished to stress that the United States is a nation, as opposed to highlighting the sovereign status each state enjoys. In most of the states, the

> In 1893, the World's Fair was held in Chicago. During the six-month celebration more than 27 million people visited. Considered a tribute to Columbus's voyage 400 years before, the fair's official name was "The World's Columbian Exposition."

Nickname
"Prairie State"

Motto
"State Sovereignty, National Union"

secretary of state is the official keeper of the state's flag and seal, but he or she cannot make changes to it without the agreement of the state legislature. The Illinois General Assembly denied Tyndale's request, but he got the last word; he simply flipped the section of banner that contains the word *Sovereignty*. When you look at the banner, you will notice that that word is upside down.

Chicago is the United States' third-largest city, and Illinois is the fifth-most-populated state in the country. According to the 2000 census, there are 12,419,293 people living in Illinois.

As with Mississippi, *Illinois* was the name of a river before it became the name of a state. *Illini* is the Algonquin Indian word for "warriors" or "tribe of superior men." French explorer Sieur de La Salle encountered the Algonquians during his explorations of this region; he gave the name *Illinois* to the river he traveled on his way to the Mississippi.

Although Illinois is known for its cities and industry, its official nickname is the "Prairie State." The state sets aside the third week in September as the annual Illinois Prairie Week. The ground that appears in the state seal, beneath the eagle and above the state name, represents prairie land—yet another way residents have paid homage to the great prairies of the Midwest.

Alabama

Alabama

Admitted

December 14, 1819

One year and two weeks after Illinois joined the Union in December 1818, the United States Congress saw fit to also add a southern state. Although the slavery issue was not yet a crucial component in deciding whether or not to grant statehood, it is interesting to note that starting with Tennessee in 1796 and ending with Maine in 1820, the admittance of states into the Union proceeded as follows: slave state (Tennessee), free state (Ohio), slave state (Louisiana), free state (Indiana), slave state (Mississippi), free state (Illinois), slave state (Alabama), free state (Maine), and slave state (Missouri). The United States was in an era of expansion where the designation "slave state" or "free state" was of the utmost importance.

It was in this atmosphere, thirty years after the United States Constitution was drafted, that Alabama was granted statehood. The date was December 14, 1819, and the nation was now twenty-two states strong.

Like Louisiana, Alabama existed under several national flags before flying a flag of its own: Spain, then France, then Great Britain, followed by the United States, the Confederate States of America, and then the American flag once more. Álonso Alvarez de Piñeda was the first European to see Alabama. He sailed for Spain and is credited with flying the first flag over the area, just as he had done in Louisiana. The French flag arrived with the explorer most closely associated with the Mississippi River, Sieur de La Salle. After the

Four significant African-American leaders were born in Alabama. They are agriculturalist and educator George Washington Carver and civil rights leaders Reverend Dr. Martin Luther King, Jr., Coretta Scott King, and Rosa Parks, whose defiance led to the Montgomery Bus Boycott.

Four important African-American athletes were also born in Alabama. Hall of Fame baseball player Willie Mays and all-time home-run king Hank Aaron were both born here, as was boxer Joe Louis. Jesse Owens, who shocked the world and all of Nazi Germany with his track and field heroics at the 1936 Olympics, also had Alabama roots.

French and Indian War, France ceded land that included Alabama to Great Britain. With the success of the American Revolutionary War, Alabama would never again have to fly a European flag.

In 1861, the United States was preparing to embark on its most tragic war. Alabama's first official flag, designed by a group of women from Montgomery, was adopted during this period of turmoil and secession. This flag was dubbed the "Secession Convention Flag," because it was adopted at the state's 1861 Secession Convention. The more common name for the flag, though, was the "Republic of Alabama Flag." It featured the goddess Liberty on the obverse (front) side of the flag. In her right hand, she held an unsheathed sword. In her left hand, she held a small flag with one star on it. The phrase "Independent Now and Forever" appeared in an arch above Liberty.

> **Much like the United States, Alabama has an official salute for its flag. It is much shorter than the Pledge of Allegiance but is a legal decree nonetheless: "Flag of Alabama I salute thee. To thee I pledge my allegiance, my service, and my life."**

On the reverse side of the flag was a cotton plant, and beneath that, a coiled rattlesnake. At the bottom of the flag was a warning in Latin: *"Noli Me Tangere,"* or "Touch Me Not." Cotton has long been Alabama's most important crop. In the early days of the twentieth century, the boll weevil, a corn-devouring insect, forced Alabama farmers to start planting peanuts instead of cotton, but it is cotton that is most closely associated with Alabama. And it was cotton that slaves picked on Alabama's plantations. This is how slavery came to be such an important part of the southern economy.

The Republic of Alabama Flag flew over the state until February 10, 1861, when it was moved to the Governor's Office after being damaged in a storm. Soon thereafter, Alabama began to fly the Confederate flag, and the original state flag was never flown again. Two Confederate flags flew over Alabama until 1865, when the United States flag returned to its proper place. Thirty years later, Alabama would adopt its second official state flag.

Alabama's new flag was designed in 1891. Four years later, on February 16, 1895, the Alabama Legislature adopted the flag. According to the *Acts of*

Nicknames

"Cotton State"
"Cotton Plantation State "
"Yellowhammer State"
"Lizard State"
"Heart of Dixie"

Motto

"We Dare Defend Our Rights"

Alabama, 1895, this flag would feature the crimson cross of St. Andrew set against a field of white. These crimson lines would "extend diagonally across the flag from side to side" and "were not to be less than six inches broad." This flag accomplishes all four of Flagman's rules: It is one of the simplest designs of all the state flags; it offers both color and distinctiveness; and includes symbolism.

The design is patterned after that of the Confederate Battle Flag. This new flag, the flag that has flown ever since 1895, is a reminder of Alabama's independent roots, as is the state's motto: *"Audemus jua nostra defendere."* This Latin phrase translates to "We Dare Defend Our Rights." And dare Alabamans have.

> **Every Christmas, tens of thousands of people crowd into the small town of Demopolis for the "Christmas on the River Cook-off." This barbecue contest employs upwards of seventy-five judges.**

> **Alabama's nicknames include the "Cotton State," the "Cotton Plantation State," the "Yellowhammer State," and the "Lizard State." Perhaps the most popular nickname among Alabamans is the "Heart of Dixie." Montgomery is the state capital and also served as the first capital of the Confederate States of America. The Constitution of the Confederacy was written and adopted in Montgomery, and Jefferson Davis took his oath of office there. This is where the nickname the "Heart of Dixie" originated.**

Maine

Maine

Admitted

March 15, 1820

Maine, known as the "Pine Tree State," was once a part of Massachusetts. It is the biggest state in all of New England. Tucked away in the northeast corner of the United States, the New England region is made up of Connecticut, Maine, Massachusetts, New Hampshire, Rhode Island, and Vermont. People from New England are often called "Yankees."

The War of 1812, coupled with the growing debate over slavery, hastened Maine's bid for statehood. Residents of the state were not happy with the lack of military protection they were receiving from Massachusetts during America's second war with Great Britain (the War of 1812). On top of that, many of Maine's residents had more liberal political viewpoints than their neighbors to the south. However, during this time it was not easy to gain acceptance into the Union. The United States government was now using the slave debate as one means of evaluating states for statehood. A territory that wanted to be a state had to apply as either a slave state or a free state (as described in their state constitution). Based on several factors, including the state's population (at least 60,000 citizens) and its status as a slave or free state, Congress would decide whether to grant statehood.

After admitting Alabama to the Union in 1819, the country had an equal number of slave states and free states. To try and keep the nation fairly balanced, when they admitted the southern state of Missouri, Congress also granted statehood to Maine (as a free state) on March 15, 1820. This congressional decision to keep the states equal, coupled with a decision to not allow slavery in any of the new states in the North, was known as the "Missouri Compromise."

> **When people think of Maine, they think of lobsters. Asked to choose another food from Maine, they would probably say potatoes. But right up there with those two provisions are blueberries. Maine is actually America's number-one producer of blueberries. While Irish immigrants first brought the potato to the state, blueberries have always grown in the wild there.**

The Missouri Compromise was important because it took control out of the states' hands. After the Kansas-Nebraska Act of 1854 overturned the Missouri Compromise, states that were south of the line of latitude at 36°30'N could once again decide for themselves whether or not to allow slavery. This is yet another example of federalism in the United States.

So it was that in 1820 Maine became our twenty-third state. The current state flag, though, was not adopted until 1909. Maine's first flag, adopted on March 21,1901, featured a pine tree and a star on a field of buff. On February 23, 1909, the 74th Maine Legislature adopted a new design that included the coat of arms (or state seal). In 1991, and again in 1997, a bill to revert to the original flag was proposed but failed to pass through the legislation. The decision to place the state's coat of arms on a field of blue has otherwise gone unchallenged since the flag's adoption in 1909, eighty-nine years after Maine was granted statehood.

> **Authors Stephen King, Henry Wadsworth Longfellow, Harriet Beecher Stowe, and E.B. White have all called Maine home.**

By incorporating the coat of arms into the new design, Maine carried on the tradition of using the pine tree as a symbol. The coat of arms features a shield; inside the shield is a pine tree with a moose beneath, resting in the shade. Above the shield is the state motto, the Latin word *"Dirigo,"* which means "I Lead." Above the motto is the North Star, long a guiding light for sailors. To the right of the shield is a sailor with an anchor, in tribute to Maine's extensive coastline, the lobstermen and the fishermen, and the wooden ship-building industry that at one point flourished here along the Atlantic Ocean. Maine's coastline is actually one of America's longest, measuring more than 3,500 miles.

To the left of the shield is a farmer holding a small scythe. This is a nod to Maine's long agricultural tradition and to the potatoes and other crops that are harvested throughout the state. Beneath the shield is a light blue banner with "Maine" boldly printed therein. The state statute also describes the other details of the flag: ". . . the edges to be trimmed with knotted fringe of yellow silk, two and one-half inches wide; a cord, with tassels, to be attached to the staff at the spearhead, to be eight feet six inches long and composed of white and blue strands." In many states, not only is the height of the staff prescribed, the style of the base and/or the top of the staff is a part of the law. In Delaware, the base of the governor's staff must be a blue hen.

The moose can be found in a number of our northern states. In Maine, this member of the deer family is honored as the state's official animal. It is therefore fitting that the moose appears on Maine's state flag. Moose can also be seen on many state road signs; if you drive through Maine, chances are you are going to see more than one moose-crossing sign. These animals are so big that in an accident, state troopers usually worry more about the car than the moose!

Unlike other states, it was not the British, Spanish, French, or Italians who first set foot on the land that would be Maine. It was around 900 A.D. that Norsemen, the Vikings of Scandinavia, first visited the region. These explorers lived along the coastlines of Europe and were constantly sailing in search of wealth and adventure. The Norsemen did not stay in Maine, though, and it was not until the 1500s that Europeans would return to American soil.

Missouri

Missouri

Admitted

August 10, 1821

The geography of the United States changed drastically in 1803. Napoléon Bonaparte, the emperor of France, accepted $15 million for Louisiana territory, and the land that would someday become Missouri was added to our quickly expanding nation. Thomas Jefferson knew that this was a deal he could not resist. What with the acquisition of the Mississippi River and the Great Plains of the Midwest, this was one of the most important—albeit easy—decisions that any United States president would ever make. What Jefferson saw, in particular, was an area that would be the nation's portal to the west. This portal was Missouri.

In St. Louis stands a tall, arching monument of steel—a symbol of this portal. This tribute to westward expansion is called, appropriately enough, The Arch. St. Louis is just one of the many cities on the Mississippi River, but its strategic position made it an important starting point for many pioneers. The Missouri River runs east-west, while the Mississippi runs north-south, and these two mighty rivers meet near St. Louis. Jefferson was right in thinking that Missouri was valuable territory; like Illinois, it offered many opportunities for travel and shipping. The Mississippi River connected Missouri with the South while the Missouri River connected the eastern part of the state with the western part and points beyond—in particular, the West's newest city, Kansas City. Other towns blossomed in the region, and by the late 1800s, railroad tracks crisscrossed the state, allowing for greater shipping and transportation between the East and the West.

Despite having the seventeenth-largest population in the nation Missouri is a very homogeneous (from a Latin word meaning "everyone the same") state, in terms of ethnicity. According to the 2000 census, eighty-five percent of the population is white. This is a much higher percentage than for the United States as a whole. Seventy-five percent of our country's population is white. The male-female split in Missouri is much more even: it is almost fifty percent women and fifty percent men.

After four years of waiting for Congressional and presidential approval, Missouri became the twenty-fourth state on August 10, 1821. Twenty-four stars are featured not once, but twice, on the state flag. In the center are twenty-four stars encircling the state seal. Twenty-four additional stars appear within the seal, above the other images. The cloud around these inner stars represents the difficulty Missouri had in attaining statehood. One star is larger than the rest; this twenty-fourth star represents Missouri.

Although this flag does not follow the Flagman's rule of simplicity, it does include several symbolic images. The two grizzly bears standing beneath the star-filled sky, and on either side of the shield, represent courage. On the right side of the shield, a bald eagle holds an olive branch of peace as well as an arrow of war in its talons; this is meant to symbolize America. The left side of the shield represents Missouri. This division of the shield is in recognition of America's system of federalism. In the upper left corner of this divided shield is a crescent moon, a representation of Missouri at the time of its statehood: small, but full of vast potential. In the lower left corner is another grizzly bear, reaffirming the strength and bravery of Missouri's citizens. Around this divided shield is the phrase "United We Stand, Divided We Fall," another reference to the strife that gripped the nation during Missouri's first few years.

> **Missouri's nickname, immortalized on the state license plates for years, is the "Show Me State." It speaks of common sense and stubbornness. "If you know how it should be done then show me!"**

It was the Missouri Compromise that allowed the federal government to decide whether a state would join the Union as a slave state or a free state. Even though Missouri entered the Union as a slave state, the state's motto is the Latin *"Salus Populi Suprema Lex Esto"* ("The Welfare of the People Shall Be the Supreme Law"). On the flag, the two grizzly bears stand on a scroll that displays this motto. Below the scroll is "MDCCCXX," or 1820 written in Roman numerals. Instead of citing 1821, the year of statehood, Missouri pays tribute to the year of the Missouri Compromise, which enabled it to finally become a member of the United States. Missouri was granted statehood in 1821 but did not have an official flag until March 22, 1913. The flag was designed by Marie Elizabeth Watkins Oliver, the wife of a Missouri senator.

The flag's field pays homage to Missouri's French roots. France's claim to the region was based on Sieur de la Salle's exploration in 1682. The land was later sold to the United States as a part of the Louisiana Purchase. Although the French flag's red, white, and blue stripes appear vertically, while Missouri's appear horizontally, the colors are a direct reproduction, and recognition, of the first flag to be raised over Missouri.

Do you know what crop farmers in Missouri are most apt to grow? Not corn, not wheat, but soybeans. The largest cash crop in the state, soybeans can be consumed by humans and animals—and can also be used in fertilizer, paint, soap, plastics, and ink.

Like many other states, Missouri derives its name from the Native Americans who once occupied the land, the Missouri Indians. These native Missourians share their name with the major waterway that passes through the state, the Missouri River. (The Mississippi River does not pass *through* the state; it serves as its western border.) *Missouri* is the Algonquian word for "river of the big canoes."

Kansas City is well known for jazz but also for its steakhouses, in part due to the livestock industry in the nearby prairie lands. Missouri is one of the United States' most important agricultural states. There are more than 100,000 farms all across Missouri.

Arkansas

97

Arkansas

Admitted

June 15, 1836

On June 15, 1836, Arkansas became the twenty-fifth state to join the Union. The United States was now halfway to being complete: in the rearview mirror was everyone from Delaware to Missouri and up ahead lay everyone from Michigan to Hawaii.

Nineteen-thirteen was a good year for state flags. Both Missouri and Arkansas adopted their official state flags that year. Arkansas paid tribute in its flag design to its status as the twenty-fifth state by surrounding the state's name with twenty-five white stars. These stars are set within a diamond-shaped border of blue. Missouri uses stars in the same pattern and colors and Georgia, Indiana, Kansas, Missouri, Nevada, North Dakota, Ohio, Oregon, and Rhode Island all demonstrate their place in American history by including a specific number of stars on their flags.

Within the flag's perimeter of stars, a diamond-shaped field of white plays host to the state's name. The diamond appears twice on the flag because Arkansas, a state that relies heavily on mining, is the only place in the United States where diamonds have ever been found. Above the state name is a lone blue star, representing Arkansas's place in the Confederacy; it entered the Union as a slave state and seceded in 1861. During the "War Between the States," approximately 60,000 Arkansans fought for the South, and 15,000 fought for the North. Beneath the state name are three blue stars representing Spain, France, and the United States, the three nations that have ruled the land that is now Arkansas. These countries all played an important role in the discovery and settlement of several southern states. The flag's field is red, completing a red, white, and blue color scheme that was chosen in tribute to the United States.

Sports teams from the University of Arkansas are nicknamed the "Razorbacks." The state's official nickname, though, is the "Natural State," due to all of Arkansas's wonderful natural resources and places of rest and recreation. Of particular note is its abundance of lakes, streams, and rivers (including the Arkansas and the Mississippi Rivers).

The first Europeans to set foot in Arkansas were the Spanish. Hernando de Soto, a Spanish conquistador, led an expedition through the region in 1541. The French explorers Marquette and Joliet explored the Mississippi River in 1673, and in 1682 Sieur de La Salle claimed for France the land that would someday be Arkansas. The first permanent European settlement was established there in 1686, and France controlled the area until 1762 when they ceded their Louisiana Territory to Spain. In 1800, Spain returned Louisiana to France. These two French-Spanish treaties are the same secret treaties that affected Louisiana. The United States took control of Arkansas in 1804, after the completion of the Louisiana Purchase.

Just as Spain, France, and Great Britain were present during the early years of many of the American states, the Daughters of the American Revolution were present for the creation of quite a few of the state flags. They would play a role in Arkansas, as well.

The state had no flag to present to the battleship USS *Arkansas* upon its commission in 1912. So, Arkansas's Daughters of the American Revolution decided to hold a statewide flag design contest. A committee of judges, including Secretary of State Earl Hodges, a professor, a teacher, and several others, selected from sixty-five entries. The flag they chose was designed by Miss Willie Hocker and was slightly different from the flag we see today. The original lacked the state's name, and the interior stars (there were only three stars in Miss Hocker's flag) were not arranged around a white diamond. But at least the state finally had a flag. The USS *Arkansas* graciously received its gift in 1913, before taking to the seas, and one year later the flag was officially adopted by the state.

In 1923, Arkansas's legislators made a change to the flag. Wishing to acknowledge not only Spain, France, and the United States but also the Confederate States of America, the General Assembly decided to add the blue star that sits above the *Arkansas*. After all, the Confederacy had been a country,

> **The capital of Arkansas is Little Rock. The name comes from a stone outcropping on the bank of the Arkansas River. This Little Rock was a landmark used by travelers, as was Big Rock, just upstream.**

Nickname

"Natural State"

Motto

"The People Rule"

and Arkansas had flown its flag. By 1924, this new and improved flag was adopted. It has not changed since.

Like the state itself, the name *Arkansas* has both French and Native American roots. The local Quapaw Indians, who lived on the lower Arkansas River near the Mississippi, were also known by the name *Akansea,* meaning "south wind." The French spelling was first seen in the *Arkansas Gazette,* and the appropriate pronunciation was thought to be AR-kan-SAW. However, a state senator argued that the name should be pronounced Ar-KAN-sas. Arkansas's General Assembly officially declared, in a state statue in 1881, that the word should indeed be pronounced differently from the spelling. They opted for the French pronunciation; thus Arkansas is said AR-kan-SAW. It's interesting to note, however, that residents of Arkansas are referred to as Arkansans, pronounced Ar-KAN-sans.

Arkansas has an official state creed which was adopted in 1972: "I believe in Arkansas as a land of opportunity and promise. I believe in the rich heritage of Arkansas and I honor the men and women who created this heritage. I believe in the youth of Arkansas who will build our future. I am proud of my state. I will uphold its constitution, obey its laws, and work for the good of all its citizens."

Michigan

In 1835, two years before Michigan achieved state status, state legislators approved a design for a Michigan state seal. Fur trading brought many people to the area, and the state's seal is based loosely on the seal of the Hudson Bay Fur Company. The state seal's design reflects the natural beauty and patriotism of the region. The most prominent image is a bald eagle; in one talon the bird grips the olive branches of peace and in the other the three arrows of war. The symbolism of the eagle seems to be peace until we (meaning America) feel war is necessary. The eagle appears, wings outspread, between an elk and a moose that are standing on their hind legs. These hoofed creatures represent Michigan while the eagle represents the United States of America. Michigan is only one of many states to portray federalism in its seal and flag.

Beneath the eagle and between the elk and moose sits a shield. It features an image of a man standing on a peninsula, next to a body of water, with the sun setting behind him. Though the exact meaning of the design is unknown, it is possible that the water is Lake Michigan and that the peninsula is that broad expanse of land that is referred to as the "U.P.," or Upper Peninsula.

> **Michigan has two nicknames. The "Great Lakes State" speaks for itself. In addition to bordering on four of the Great Lakes, Michigan is home to thousands of smaller lakes.**
>
> **The story of Michigan's other nickname, the "Wolverine State," is more complicated. Legend has it that residents of Ohio dubbed their neighbors "wolverines" during the 1830s. Others say that the nickname was created by local Native Americans during that same period. In both cases, possession of land was at the heart of the confrontations. In short, the settlers in the Michigan Territory fought like wolverines to protect their land claims. Although the nickname was originally intended as a criticism, Michiganians have embraced it. Today, sports teams from the University of Michigan go by the name "Wolverines."**

Michigan is divided into two distinct parcels of land, the Upper and Lower Peninsulas; between them is Lake Michigan.

In the man's left hand is a gun. He is gripping the barrel like a walking stick, holding it in a nonconfrontational manner as he raises his other hand in greeting. The message is peaceful but with the reminder that he will defend his rights if he has to. One of the rights exerted by the United States during the 1830s was the right of expansion. Within a few years, Manifest Destiny would become standard policy, and territories upon territories would fall under American control.

The country was growing as if by divine right, as if the government's decisions were best for all. Although Native Americans argued this point with their lives, immigrants were pouring into New York City and other ports, and America's leaders believed that it was important to establish and protect, settle, and eventually grant statehood to the territories of the West.

Michigan joined the Union as a free state, meaning that it did not support slavery. The mottoes that appear on the state seal reflect this libertarian philosophy. *"Si Quaeris Peninsulam Amoenam Circumspice"* stretches between the elk and moose. These words, scrolled on a white banner in Latin, translate to "If you seek a pleasant peninsula, look about you."

"E Pluribus Unum" is possibly the most famous, and most often used, Latin quote in the United States. It is our nation's motto (adopted in 1782) and has been featured on the Great Seal of the United States of America since 1776 when Benjamin Franklin, John Adams, Thomas Jefferson and the rest of the Great Seal committee placed it there. *"E Pluribus Unum"* means "Out of many, one" and refers to the United States being one nation of many states, and many people, bonded together in the defense of freedom and justice. This motto can be found above the bald eagle on the Michigan state seal.

"Tuebor" ("I will defend") appears above the head of the waving man with the gun; again the man seems to proclaim that Michigan will fight to defend its wants and needs.

Nicknames

"Great Lakes State"
"Wolverine State"

Motto

"If You Seek a Pleasant Peninsula, Look About You"

Michigan became our twenty-sixth state on January 26, 1837. Later that year the state's General Assembly adopted the first of three state flags. This first flag utilized the state seal along with three additional images. On the back side of the flag was a portrait of the state's first governor, Stevens T. Mason (the only actual person, other than George Washington, to ever appear on a state flag). On the front, or obverse, side were a woman and a soldier, along with the state seal. In 1865, the flag's obverse side was simplified and the woman and soldier were removed, allowing the flag to come closer to attaining the rule of simplicity discussed in the Introduction. Michigan's flag would simply consist of the state seal on a field of blue. On the reverse side, former Governor Mason was removed and the United States coat of arms was added, possibly in tribute to Michigan's allegiance in the Civil War. In 1911, Michigan adopted its third and current flag. Its appearance was similar to the previous flag, minus the federal government's coat of arms.

> The 2000 census showed that Michigan is the eighth-most-populated state in the United States. With 96,810 square miles of land (Michigan is the eleventh biggest state) there is plenty of room for the 9,938,444 residents of the state.

> Michigan has a longer coastline than any other state except Alaska. There is almost as much water as land in Michigan, due to the presence of four of the Great Lakes (Lake Michigan, Lake Erie, Lake Huron, and Lake Superior), Lake St. Clair, and several rivers.

Florida

Florida

Admitted

March 3, 1845

For eight years in the late 1830s, the United States took a break from allowing territories to join the Union. The slave-state-versus-free-state debate was in full swing, and after Florida's white male citizens voted to petition for statehood, the 28th Congress finally made its decision, passing the "Act for Admission" on December 2, 1844. All that is required after an act of admission is the president's signature. By 1845, President James Polk had signed both Florida and Texas into statehood. To balance the addition of these southern slave states, Congress and the president soon granted state status to Iowa and Wisconsin in the North.

The Spanish played an important role in Florida's early history. Juan Ponce de León sailed to the New World with Christopher Columbus in 1493. Twenty years later, Ponce de León led an expedition of his own. In 1513, he landed on the coast of Florida; most historians, citing a lack of proof that Norsemen ever landed in the northeast, say that he was the first European to set foot in North America. During this time, the Spanish flag was the only banner to fly over Florida.

It was Ponce de León who named the new colony "La Florida," in honor of the Spanish celebration Pascua Florida (or the "feast of the flowers"). Ponce de León was killed by Native Americans during his second expedition to La Florida. He had spent the better part of his life searching for the Fountain of

Florida may be America's twenty-eighth-smallest state, but it is the fourth-most-populated, behind New York, Texas, and California. Florida's population has increased more than twenty-three percent since the 1990 census.

Why do so many people call this thin peninsula home? Tourism is the state's leading industry and employer. The population also includes many retirees who flock to Florida for the forgiving tax laws. The support services that go along with an aging population also attract younger residents; nurses and other caregivers can find work here in one of the nation's fastest-growing job markets. Whatever their reason, nearly sixteen million people call the "Sunshine State" home.

Youth. Floridians actually celebrate a State Day (April 2) in honor of the (approximate) day that Ponce de León found the colony. It was a social studies teacher, Mary A. Harrell, who first suggested this event.

After the Spanish flag, Florida saw the French flag, the "Union Jack" of Great Britain, the three Confederate States of America flags, and the flag of the United States raised overhead. There were also several unofficial state flags before the first appearance of the state seal on a white banner, which served as the state flag from 1868 to 1890. Toward the turn of the nineteenth century, Florida Governor Francis P. Fleming requested that the crimson cross of St. Andrew, which resembles a large X, be added to the design. He felt that the state flag, which was mostly white, looked too much like the traditional flag of surrender.

Florida's state flag is very similar to Alabama's. While both utilize the crimson cross of St. Andrew, the Florida flag still includes the state seal, centered over the cross. Florida state legislators adopted this state seal in 1868. The original seal included images of a ship, a cocoa tree, and rays of sunlight in the background, and a Native American woman scattering flowers in the foreground. These images were encircled by the words "Great Seal of the State of Florida: In God We Trust." This seal was placed on the flag, along with the cross of St. Andrew, and the flag was adopted in 1890.

In 1953, Florida's General Assembly named the Sabal palmetto palm tree its official state tree, and in 1970 the cocoa tree on the state flag was changed to a palmetto (the palmetto also appears on the South Carolina flag). Other changes were also made at this time. The Native American woman's clothing was changed and her feathered headdress removed so that she would look more like a Seminole Indian; ancestors of the Seminoles have lived in Florida

> **The state marine mammal is the beloved manatee. Manatees are also sometimes referred to as sea cows although they are most closely related to the elephant. A full grown manatee can weigh more than 1,000 pounds. Despite their size, legend has it that sailors used to think that manatees were mermaids.**

Nickname
"Sunshine State"

Motto
"In God We Trust"

for thousands of years. The mountain was removed from the background, and the ship was altered.

Also in 1970, the General Assembly gave Florida the nickname the "Sunshine State." The rays of sunlight still appear on the state seal and the state flag. According to Florida law, the state seal must be the size of an American silver dollar, on the flag it must be "in diameter one-half the hoist," and it "shall occupy the center of a white ground." Whatever changes the state seal may undergo, so shall the flag. By state statute, the state seal (the most *current* state seal) shall forever grace the state flag.

Today, more than 2,000 Seminoles live on six reservations around the state. They call themselves the "Unconquered People" because they are all the descendents of the 300 Seminoles who survived the Indian Removal Programs of the 1800s.

St. Augustine was established in 1565 by Pedro Menéndez de Avilés, a Spanish explorer. The city was built on the site of the Native American village where Ponce de León had landed in 1513. St. Augustine has endured attacks by the British, the Seminoles, and settlers from South Carolina and Georgia—it was even occupied by Union soldiers during the Civil War—to become the oldest city in the United States.

Texas

Admitted

December 29, 1845

exans take pride in their independence, referring to their state as the "Lone Star State." For a time, Texas, like Vermont, was an independent nation. It even fought its own war against Mexico. Later, when the United States annexed (took possession of) Texas, Texans fought in the Mexican-American War.

Texas has seen a number of flags throughout its history. From 1519 to 1685, the flag of Spain flew overhead. Then, Sieur de La Salle planted the French flag on Texas soil. It flew there, near the Gulf of Mexico, for only five years. Fighting with Native Americans mixed with infighting—one of La Salle's own men murdered him—and quickly led to the end of the French presence. After they departed, the Spanish began to establish missions throughout the region, including one that they named Francisco de los Tejas. *Tejas* means "friends" and eventually its anglicized form became the name of our twenty-eighth state.

The Spanish flag continued to fly until 1821, when Mexico gained their independence from Spain. So, from 1821 to 1836 the Mexican flag was dominant in Texas. When Santa Anna declared himself dictator of Mexico in 1836, Texas broke off relations with that country. Sam Houston became the president of the Republic of Texas and approved the symbol that is still known as the Lone Star Flag. Its bold design included a blue vertical stripe one-third the flag's width and two horizontal stripes, one red and one white. Within the blue stripe was a single white star.

On December 29, 1845, Texas ceased to be independent and joined the Union. The United States Congress, in an effort to balance the admission of the free states of Iowa and Wisconsin, accepted Texas as a slave state. The Lone Star flag flew along with the American flag (except during the Civil War)

According to the 2000 census, the population of Texas is 20,851,820. This was an increase of 22 percent since 1990. It should be no surprise to learn, then, that Texas is the second-largest (behind Alaska) and the second-most-populous (behind California) state in the country.

until 1879 when Texas legislators repealed the statutes that described their flag. It was not until 1933 that Texas passed its Flag Act, describing the design of the flag, including the official colors (blood red, azure blue, and white) and the exact location of the star.

In 2001, the Texas House of Representatives made official the rules of care and retirement for their beloved flag. Title 11, Subchapter D, Section 3100.151 reads:

"I am your Texas flag! I was born January 25, 1839. I am one of only two flags of an American state that has also served as the symbol of an independent nation—The Republic of Texas. While you may honor me in retirement, the spirit I represent will never retire! I represent the spirit of Texas—Yesterday, Today, and Tomorrow!

"I represent the bravery of the Alamo and the Victory at San Jacinto. My spirit rode with the Texas Rangers over the Forts Trail of the Big Country and herded cattle through the Fort Worth stockyards. I have sailed up Galveston Bay and kept a watchful eye over our El Paso del Norte. My colors are in the waters of the Red River and in the Bluebonnets of the Texas Hill Country. You'll find my spirit at the Light House of Palo Duro and in the sands of Padre Island; I am in the space station at Houston and atop the oil wells of West Texas. From the expanse of the Big Bend to the Riverwalk of San Antone—all of Texas is my home! I wave over the cotton and grain fields of the High Plains, and I am deep in the rich soil of the Rio Grande Valley. I am proudly displayed under the Capitol Dome, and I fly high above the concrete canyons of downtown Dallas. You'll find my spirit in the East Texas piney woods and along the Grandeur of the Rio Grande. I represent Texas—every Child, Woman, and Man!

"The blue field in me stands for the valor of our ancestors in the battles for our country. Let us retire the blue—Salute! My white field stands for the purity in all our Texas hearts! It represents the honor that each of us should pay to our state each day. Let us retire the white—Salute! The red is for all of the men and women who have died in service of our state—whether as members of the armed services or as citizen Samaritans. Let us retire the red—Salute! My lone, independent star is recognized worldwide because it represents ALL of Texas and stands for our unity as one for God, State, and Country. Let us retire the lone star—Salute!"

Nickname
"Lone Star State"

Motto
"Friendship"

Texas's flag is easily one of the most recognizable of the fifty states', with its three colors of red, white, and blue and its single star. This lone star is the symbol most often associated with the state of Texas. Texans have even gone so far as to attach meaning to each of the star's five points. Legend has it that each point represents the characteristics of a good Texan: loyalty, prudence, fortitude, broadmindedness, and righteousness. On the merits of its simplicity and colors, its symbolism and its distinctive design, Texas's Lone Star Flag earned second place in the "Great NAVA Survey of 2001"; only the flag of New Mexico scored higher. The recognition was certainly deserved.

> Texas is home to thirty-two of the forty-two species of bats found in the United States. Bats not only protect crops by eating insects, some bats even pollinate plants!

> Texas's state insect is the monarch butterfly. These butterflies live throughout North and South America, and on many Pacific Islands. Those monarch butterflies that live in colder climates can migrate up to 2,000 miles during the fall.

Iowa

113

Iowa

Admitted
December 28, 1846

It was European explorers who first came to Iowa during the late 1600s. In particular, French fur traders had an interest in the area. In 1673, Jacques Marquette and Louis Jolliet sailed the Mississippi River followed by Sieur de La Salle in 1681. In the years following the Louisiana Purchase, American troops, including troops led by a young Lt. Jefferson Davis (the future president of the Confederate States of America), protected the rights of these Native American tribes, but that ended in 1830. Two years later, the Black Hawk War began as the Fox and Sac, led by Chief Black Hawk, fought to regain their lands. By 1850, all Native American land in Iowa and Illinois was controlled by state and federal government.

Although the United States Congress approved Iowa's Act of Admission (it was approved along with the Act of Admission for Florida) in December 1844, President James Polk did not sign Iowa into statehood until 1846. Although there were debates at the congressional level, some of the barriers to achieving state status actually came from within the territory itself. Territorial Governor Robert Lucas had pushed for statehood for years; Iowa's population had been increasing rapidly, and many in Congress felt that it was a prime candidate to join the Union. However, the majority of Iowa's voters were hesitant to take on the cost of running a state government (the federal government supported territorial governments). The people of Iowa rejected two proposals before finally approving a state constitution that included a petition for statehood.

Within the United States Congress there was still some dispute over Iowa's boundaries, but these were soon resolved. Iowa was welcomed into the Union as a free state on December 28, 1846, one of nine states to have been

> As with Mississippi, Ohio, Illinois, and Wisconsin, Iowa was named after a river. The state was named for the Iowa River, which was named by local Native Americans (the *Ioway* tribe). The French and English called these Native Americans the "Iowa Indians." There are several interpretations of the word Iowa; some say it means "the beautiful land" or "this is the place."

granted statehood during this month. This makes December the most popular month for Congress to pass their Act of Admission legislation along to the president. While Missouri was not admitted to the Union in December, it does have two things in common with Iowa. Both states were acquired from France as part of the Louisiana Purchase. And, not surprisingly, both states have flags that are reminiscent of the French flag. Missouri's red, white, and blue stripes run horizontally, while Iowa's run vertically just as they do on the French flag.

Also like several other state flags, Iowa's features a bald eagle. The national symbol can be seen spreading its wings in an intimidating manner on a field of white. In the bird's beak is a banner reading "Our Liberties We Prize and Our Rights We Will Maintain," Iowa's state motto.

In keeping with this motto, Iowa was accepted into the Union as a free state. However, the people had to take action to ensure that liberty was maintained for all in Iowa. The Missouri Compromise had enabled acceptance into the Union as a free state, but when the 1854 Kansas-Nebraska Act overturned this act, many Iowans worried that slavery might become legal. They elected a new governor, James Grimes, who was instrumental in organizing the state's antislavery Republican Party. With their votes, Iowans reiterated, "Our rights we will maintain."

The bald eagle and its banner also appear on the Great Seal of Iowa, which Iowa's legislators adopted in 1847. This is the only detail that the flag and seal share. Beneath the banner on the flag is the state name in red capital letters.

During World War I, a group of National Guardsmen from Iowa lamented the lack of a flag to represent their home state. Other National Guard regiments had state flags to fly, and Iowa's regiment needed a flag to distinguish their unit from others. Not only was there a need for recognition, at this point

> A small group of German immigrants came to Iowa in the 1840s in search of religious freedom. The **Amana Church Society** is the corporate name of their group of communal villages, which still exist today. These people are famous for their farms and the blankets they sell. The Amana Church Society includes fewer than one thousand citizens today.

Nickname
"Hawkeye State"

State motto
"Our Liberties We Prize and Our Rights We Will Maintain"

Iowa had been a state for over seventy-five years. The time had come. The National Guardsmen wrote to their legislators and, as happened in other states, the Daughters of the American Revolution came to the rescue: they called for a state flag contest. In 1917, one of the DAR's members, Dixie Cornell Gebhardt of Knoxville, Iowa, designed the winning flag. She chose the French colors, but had her own symbolic reasons for each. Mrs. Gebhardt intended the blue stripe to represent loyalty, justice, and truth; the white stripe to stand for purity; and the red stripe to signify courage. The Iowa General Assembly officially adopted her design in 1921 and the state flag has not changed since.

> **During the 1930s, George Nissen, of Cedar Rapids, invented the trampoline. Not only was it used for recreation, Navy pilots used the trampoline as part of their flight training.**

> **Des Moines is Iowa's largest city. The population in 2000 was 198,682 people. Iowa is one of the smaller states; fewer than three million people call it home. And here's an amazing statistic: only fifty-two people per square mile live there. All of this makes Iowa the twentieth-smallest of the states. Based on its population, Iowa is represented in the United States Congress by five representatives and has seven electoral votes.**
>
> **At the state level, the General Assembly has a senate with fifty members and a house of representatives with one hundred members.**

Wisconsin

Although the patriotic colors of red, white, and blue are used in many of the state flags, the most popular color for the field (or background) is the dark shade of blue seen on the United States flag. This blue is meant to represent loyalty. More than half of the fifty state flags use a shade of blue to back their flag. In Wisconsin, the state flag features a "background of royal blue cloth" according to state statue, adopted in 2000. The state coat of arms appears on both the obverse (front) and reverse (back) sides of the flag, centered on this "royal blue cloth."

Above Wisconsin's coat of arms is a small white banner with "Forward" written in black. Adopted in 1851, "Forward" is the state motto and is indicative of Wisconsin's drive to be a leader of states within the nation. Above the banner, in much larger white block letters, appears "Wisconsin." Beneath the banner rests the state animal, the badger. (The badger is also the nickname of the sports teams at the University of Wisconsin, located in the capital city of Madison.) Beneath the badger is the coat of arms.

Wisconsin's coat of arms, like that in most states, is in the form of a shield. This shield is divided into four sections. Navigation, manufacturing, mining, and agriculture are all represented by the tools of those trades. These are drawn in dark blue—darker than the field—against the yellow background of the shield. On the right side of the shield stands a miner with a pickax in his left hand. On the left is a sailor holding a coil of rope in his right hand. These men represent the working people of Wisconsin.

Beneath the shield sits a pyramid built with thirteen ingots of lead, representing Wisconsin's vast mineral resources. The number thirteen was chosen

Dotting Wisconsin's landscape are hundreds of dairy farms. As a matter of fact, Wisconsin is America's leading producer of cheese. Milk is the state's official beverage, the dairy cow is the state's official domestic animal, and Wisconsin's people are often referred to as Cheeseheads. Watch a Green Bay Packers game, and you will quickly spot dozens of triangular cheesehead hats in the crowd!

in reference to the original thirteen colonies. To the left of this pyramid is a cornucopia, for all of Wisconsin's farm products.

Since this flag is so similar in color and style to the flags of many other states, Wisconsin's leaders decided to add the name and date of statehood. In 1979, the year "1848" was added to the bottom of the flag, and the large "Wisconsin" was placed at the top of the flag; both are written in white. These were the first changes made to the flag since 1913. Although a flag flown by certain Wisconsin regiments during the Civil War had generally been accepted as the state flag, it was not until 1913 that state legislators adopted an official flag.

Wisconsin ranks fourth in the country in terms of total water area. With its access to Lakes Michigan and Superior, its large inland Lake Winnebago, and the Wisconsin River, the state boasts 11,190 square miles of water.

Wisconsin was the thirtieth state to join the Union. Before statehood, the land was referred to as the Wisconsin Territory. The United States gained these lands as a part of the Treaty of Ghent, which officially ended the War of 1812. Once the British ceded the land to the United States, it became a part of the Illinois Territory. For a time, Wisconsin was also considered a part of the Michigan Territory. Finally, on May 29, 1848, Wisconsin entered the Union as a free state.

The British were not the only obstacle to establishing a safe territory here for settlers. The United States fought in the Black Hawk War in 1832, defeating the Native Americans and clearing the way for settlements to be built. The land was very attractive to early pioneers; if they did not move to Wisconsin for the fur trade, they came to mine the lead. Either way, Wisconsin was growing, and in less than twenty years would become a state.

When it was discovered how rich and inexpensive Wisconsin's soil was, many European immigrants made their way out west. In particular, many Germans settled in Wisconsin so that they could continue their family tradition of farming. Another tradition they brought with them was the fall festival Oktoberfest, which is still celebrated across Wisconsin during late September and early October. Immigrants also came to the state from Ireland, Poland, and

Scandinavia. Whether to farm or to mine, to lumber or to sail, Wisconsin's settlers felt pride for their heritage, pride for their state, and pride for their new country.

The center of the state's coat of arms is a patriotic image in red, white, and blue. Above thirteen vertical

In recent years, the *Utne Reader* and the *Capital Times* have run stories indicating a groundswell of support for a new Wisconsin state flag.

stripes are the words *"E Pluribus Unum,"* or "Out of many, one." This image was included in the coat of arms to show Wisconsin's dedication to federalism and, even more so, to the United States of America.

Golda Meir, who would go on to be the first and only female prime minister of Israel, lived in Wisconsin for eleven years. She attended the state's public schools and used the knowledge she gained there to lead the Israeli people from 1969 to 1974. The prime minister is to Israel what the president is to the United States.

California

CALIFORNIA REPUBLIC

121

California

Admitted
September 9, 1850

When the United States defeated Mexico in the Mexican-American War in 1848, it was able to lay claim to the territories of Texas and California. The Gold Rush was on, and Americans by the thousands headed west. Soon California would be heavily settled and would become the thirty-first member of the United States. But first, a heated debate would take place in the United States Congress. Should California be admitted as a slave state or as a free state? At the heart of the matter was the struggle to keep the nation together.

California was such a large territory that its status as a free or slave state would greatly impact the balance in Congress. Not only did Washington, D.C., allow slavery at this time, it also was home to the largest slave market in North America. With the Compromise of 1850, the slave trade was outlawed in the nation's capital, although slavery itself was still legal. The territories of New Mexico, Nevada, Arizona, and Utah would be admitted as states in the near future, and the slavery issue would be decided within each individual state. Most damaging of all was the Fugitive Slave Act, a stipulation of the Compromise of 1850. This act made it illegal to allow escaped slaves to live free in the North. If caught, they would be returned to their owner. This was one of the trade-offs for admitting California as a free state.

California was first explored by the Englishman Sir Francis Drake, as well as two Spaniards, Juan Rodríguez Cabrillo and Sebastián Vizcaíno. It is

In California, you can swim in the ocean in the morning, ski in the mountains in the afternoon, and camp in the desert at night. The natural habitat includes the Pacific Ocean, Death Valley, and the Sierra Nevada Mountains. The highest point in the continental United States is California's Mt. Whitney, which stands at 14,491 feet above sea level. The country's lowest point is also in California; at 282 feet below sea level, Death Valley regularly sees temperatures above 100 degrees Fahrenheit. America's hottest day on record was July 10, 1913, when temperatures in Death Valley reached a sweltering 135 degrees Fahrenheit.

thought that the state's name originated in a Spanish novel, *Las Sergas de Esplandian,* written by Garcia Ordonez de Montalvo in 1510. In the book, the city of Califia holds special meaning; it is a land of many resources.

It was not until the Gold Rush that California really became a desirable place to live. The year most closely associated with the Gold Rush is 1849 (this is where the National Football League's San Francisco 49ers get their name). One year later, on September 9, 1850, California was granted statehood.

Back before people had really started to "rush" out to California, before statehood was even being considered, a group of pioneers attacked a Mexican fort at Sonoma. They took the fort's commanding officer, Mariano Vallejo, prisoner and quickly hoisted a flag that had been designed just for the occasion. One of the pioneers, William Todd, painted this makeshift flag on a cotton sheet with red and brown paint. The flag featured a grizzly bear and a lone star, along with the name "California Republic." It was raised high above the fort for all the pioneers to see.

> A bill approved on April 3, 1937 named the redwood as California's official state tree. In 1953, the state legislature clarified the law, naming both types of redwoods (the Sierra big tree and the coast redwood). These trees can live thousands of years and stand hundreds of feet tall. Most redwoods now exist on protected lands, which means they cannot be cut down.

Todd and the others were intent upon freeing California from Mexico's grip. Their actions became known as the Bear Flag Revolt because of the bear that graced the flag. To these rebels, the bear symbolized strength. The star was a reference to the Lone Star of Texas; the pioneers saw Texas as California's sister in the struggle against Mexico. This revolt took place on June 14, 1846, and the flag flew from that day until July 9, 1846, when the Mexican-American War officially began.

The American flag replaced the Bear Flag and, unfortunately, the original Bear Flag was lost during the San Francisco earthquake of 1906. It wasn't until 1911 that California's state legislature would adopt the Bear Flag as the official state flag.

Nickname
"Golden State"

Motto
"Eureka!"

The new and improved flag utilized all of the original images and words, as borrowed from the Bear Flag Revolt. The bear is depicted in detail on a white field and is seen walking across a patch of green grass. The star is now red. "California Republic" appears in the same shade of brown as the bear. There is a thin stripe of red along the bottom of the flag (perhaps to offer a splash of color when the flag hangs limp, as in the Tennessee flag).

Between the Gold Rush, the push for a transcontinental railroad, and California's proximity to Mexico, California has one of the most diverse populations of any of the states. According to the last census, only 59.5 percent of Californians are "White"; 32.4 percent are "Hispanic," 10.9 percent are "Asian," 6.7 percent are "Black," and 16.8 percent consider themselves to be "Other." More immigrants settle in California than in any other state. In 1990, these new Californians made up more than 30 percent of all immigrants to come to the United States. According to the 2000 census, California is America's most heavily populated state; almost thirty-four million people call the state home. You might say that the Gold Rush is still on.

On the heels of the Gold Rush, it should be no surprise to learn that California's state motto is "Eureka!" *Eureka* is a Greek word, meaning "I have found it." "Eureka" has appeared on the state seal since 1849 and was made the official state motto in 1963.

Minnesota

The roots of Minnesota's name can be found in its earliest citizens, the Native Americans. The Dakota Sioux named the Minnesota River, but they were not long for the region once the fur traders and pioneers arrived. In choosing its flag design, Minnesota has presented an honest depiction of the way the state was settled, but the result is a controversial image. A Native American, possibly a Sioux or an Ojibwa, rides westward as a pioneer farms what was once his land.

Originally, both the Sioux and the Ojibwa welcomed the French, who were drawn to Minnesota by the fur trade. After the War of 1812, though, these tribes had to contend with American settlers. The Ojibwa were living in the Northwest Territory, and the Sioux were situated in land ceded to the United States as a part of the Louisiana Purchase. By the time Minnesota became a territory, in 1849, the United States government had signed treaties with the two tribes and divided the land.

On May 11, 1858, Minnesota became the thirty-second state. It was added to the Union as a free state, and when the Civil War began, Minnesotans stayed with the Union. In 1862, the United States Congress signed the Homestead Act, which led to a population explosion in Minnesota; settlers were promised one hundred sixty acres of land, for a small fee, if they could develop and maintain the land for five years. This incentive was intended to develop the west and to relieve the pressure on the overpopulated cities of the East Coast.

The United States Postal Service has designated a two-letter abbreviation for each state. If you are writing a letter to someone in Minnesota, for example, you follow the name of the town with MN (and then the zip code). There are eight states that begin with the letter "M": MA (Massachusetts), MD (Maryland), ME (Maine), MI (Michigan), MO (Missouri), MS (Mississippi), and MT (Montana). Once you have memorized all of these, you can start on the "N" states. There are eight of those, too!

After the Civil War, the Sioux began to resist the United States government. They saw the treaties they had signed as a temporary bandage for a life threatening wound. So, instead of retreating west, in 1862 the Sioux sent a war party led by Chief Little Crow to attack white settlements in the region. The Sioux were defeated and removed, as other Native Americans had been in so many other states during this time, and towns and railroads began to sprout up all over Minnesota.

The centerpiece of Minnesota's flag is the state seal. On it, an interesting scene plays out. In the foreground is a farmer tilling his soil. He has stopped to watch a Native American on horseback, galloping westward. The farmer is holding his plow, but resting against a nearby stump are his gun and powder-horn, along with an axe. It is apparent that this land no longer belonged to the Sioux or the Ojibwa; it was not shared between the settlers and the Native Americans the way it would be shared by the Germans, Irish, Poles, Brits, Finns, Swedes, and Norwegians. It was this settlement that forced Native Americans westward. The state flag is a constant reminder of this aspect of American history.

With its 10,000-plus lakes, not to mention rivers such as the Mississippi, Minnesota, and St. Croix, the waters of the state bring more than two million people to fish each year.

Minnesota's flag also features three significant years, all woven in gold. Above the state seal is "1893," the year the state flag was officially adopted. In a red ribbon draped around the seal are the years "1858," the year of Minnesota's statehood; and "1819," the year in which Minnesota's Fort Snelling was established.

Below the year 1858 is the state motto, on a red banner, scrolled in gold: *"L'etoile du Nord,"* which is French for "Star of the North." Other than Alaska, Minnesota is the northernmost of the fifty United States, and one of the state's nicknames is the "North Star State." Minnesota is also known as the "Land of 10,000 Lakes." Beware the mosquitoes of Minnesota in the summer!

Surrounding the state seal is a wreath of pink and white lady's slippers, the state flower. A second ring surrounds the seal and holds nineteen stars, grouped in five clusters. These clusters create the five points of a star. The nineteen stars represent the nineteen states that were granted statehood after the original thirteen. At the top of the flag is the largest of these stars; it represents Minnesota. "Minnesota" appears in red at the bottom of this white band.

This current version of the state flag was adopted in 1957. The original state flag that had been designed in 1893 displayed a wreath of white lady's slippers. This flower is not even native to Minnesota! So, it was replaced with the native pink and white lady's slipper.

According to the Flagman's Four Rules for grading flags (see Introduction), it is important that a flag have symbolism. On this particular flag, the farmer represents Minnesota's agricultural history. The tree stump speaks to Minnesota's lumber industry. The Native American in the background certainly symbolizes the region's native population and the treatment they received from the settlers and the government. If this image can be interpreted in a negative fashion, then it is hard to say that the flag of Minnesota is beautiful. Is this figure of a Native American a tribute or just a painful reminder?

"Minnesota Blue," written in 1985 by Cordell Keith Haugen, is featured on the state's website even though it is not yet the official state poem. The following is an excerpt: "Do your golden fields of wheat and corn/Still shimmer in the early morn/Waving to the clouds as they drift by/Do moose and bear still rule the earth/In the Red River Valley of my birth/Do the Northern Lights still dance across your sky/Does the North Star still guide you?/Do your farmers still provide you/With the way of life that we all learned to share . . ."

Oregon

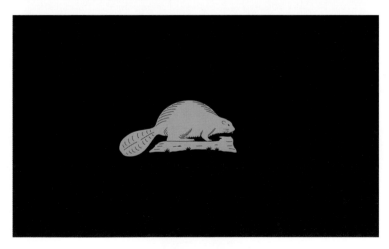

Oregon

Admitted

February 14, 1859

Oregon was the second Pacific Coast state, after California, to be admitted to the Union. As in California, Oregon's population was flourishing; the Oregon Trail led many settlers here after the United States government opened the Oregon Territory in 1848. In 1857, the territory developed its state seal, and two years later, on February 14, 1859, the United States Congress accepted Oregon's petition for statehood. Although Oregon entered the Union as a free state, its state constitution made clear that freed African-Americans would not be allowed to enter the state. This was out of respect for the sister states of the South.

Oregon's flag, which it adopted in 1925, is special for two reasons. It is the only current state flag to feature different images on the front and back. On the obverse, or front, side is a slightly altered version of the state seal. On the reverse side is the state animal, the beaver.

The colors of the official flag are gold and blue. Both the beaver and the state seal are done in gold while the flag's field is dark blue. Within the shield is a setting sun, its rays spreading out over the Pacific Ocean. In the foreground is a Conestoga wagon, the type used by many pioneers who took to the Oregon Trail. Several images on the flag speak to Oregon's natural resources: to the left of the wagon is a forest, and beneath these images are a plow, a sheaf of wheat, and a pickax. Next to the wagon is a banner that reads, "The Union." This was the state's motto when the flag was adopted, reflecting the sentiment in 1857 when the seal was designed. All of this is also done in gold.

To add to the intricate detail of the seal, two ships, one British and one American, sail the Pacific Ocean. The British ship, a man o' war, is leaving the shore, while the American ship is arriving. This was done on purpose,

> **Buffalo dung (hardened manure) had several uses for those pioneers traveling along the Oregon Trail. Not only did the dung act as a substitute for the firewood that was sometimes scarce, kids could fling these discs of dung much like a Frisbee is flung today!**

to symbolize the transference of power from Great Britain to the United States.

Perched atop the shield is a bald eagle, its wings spread protectively. Surrounding the shield, also taking the shape of a heart, are thirty-three golden stars, representing Oregon's place as the thirty-third state to join the Union.

The state seal includes the phrase "State of Oregon," along with "1859," in a circle around the shield. On the flag, "State of Oregon" appears above the shield in large gold letters, taking the shape of a banner, and "1859" appears in gold beneath the shield.

The beaver's presence on the flag is another acknowledgment of the state's natural beauty and vast resources. Beavers build their dams with small fallen trees so those that live in Oregon have certainly lucked out. Almost half of Oregon is forestland! Since 1950, our thirty-third state has provided America with the majority of its lumber and plywood. At the same time, environmentalists have made sure that much of the land goes untouched. The state boasts thirteen national forests and more than two hundred state parks.

> **Matt Groening, the cartoonist who created "The Simpsons," was born in Portland in 1954.**

Farming is another big source of income in Oregon. Among the crops grown here are peppermint, pears, strawberries, onion, broccoli, wheat, and cherries. There are even vineyards, helping to build Oregon's burgeoning wine industry. There are many livestock farms, including cattle for beef and dairy products, sheep, and poultry. There are even fur farms where mink are raised and slaughtered. Many animal activists are not happy about this and have protested against the further harm of animals.

Many of the state's animal rights and environmental activists are students in the state's extensive university system. Oregon State University is located in Corvallis; its mascot is the state animal, the beaver. The Fighting Ducks, the nickname at the University of Oregon in Eugene, is the only copyrighted image to have ever been used by one of America's universities. It was with Walt Disney's approval, in 1947, that Donald Duck became associated with the school. The university even went so far as to make Donald Duck an honorary alumnus on the fiftieth anniversary of his relationship with the school!

The year 2003 marks the two-hundredth anniversary of the Lewis and Clark Expedition. In 1803, the Louisiana Purchase doubled the size of the United States and President Thomas Jefferson quickly sent explorers Meriwether Lewis and William Clark west. President Jefferson wanted a map of these lands, and to know if there was a waterway connecting the Missouri River and the Pacific Ocean. After traveling through the lands that would someday be known as Missouri, Kansas, Nebraska, Iowa, South and North Dakota, Montana, Idaho, Washington, and Oregon, Lewis and Clark's Corps of Discovery canoed down the Columbia River which led them to their goal: the Pacific Ocean. The Columbia River is now the border between Oregon and Washington.

Oregon's beaver and the duck even have a historical connection. Before Oregon officially became the "Beaver State" in 1909, the state's nickname was the "Webfoot State." Originally, the Webfoots were Massachusetts fishermen who helped George Washington and his troops to defeat the British during the American Revolutionary War. Their descendants moved west, to Oregon, where they helped to build the fishing industry. Although fishing is no longer a real economic boon to the state, fish farms do exist, and fishing towns dot the state's beautiful coastline.

Kansas

The names *Arkansas* and *Kansas* share the same root. Both were French adaptations of Native American words, and both relate to the Kansas River. In the midst of terrible times, at the start of the Civil War in 1861, Kansas was granted statehood. Sixty-six years later, during kinder times, Kansas adopted its first state flag. As in many other states, the flag is the state seal set on a field of dark blue. This design has gone unchanged since 1927.

The Kansas flag depicts a history of peaceful coexistence between the natives of the land and the newly arrived settlers. But whether this relationship was truly peaceful is debatable. In the foreground of the state seal is a farmer plowing his field. Beyond the farmer, oxen-drawn schooners form a wagon train that is traveling westward. Beyond these pioneers are Native Americans hunting bison. Some flags have been so poorly reproduced that the Native Americans have been erased completely and, at best, a few brown smudges remain to represent the bison. This is a problem when flags are shrunk down in size. Sometimes, though, it is merely the result of poor craftsmanship (as often seen on the Internet).

The pioneers represent Manifest Destiny, which was the prevailing attitude of the United States government starting in the 1840s. The farmer and his field represent Kansas's rich agricultural history. The seal also includes a steamboat churning its way down the Kansas River, meant to represent commerce. Today manufacturing and service industries dominate the Kansas economy. Although Kansas still has its vast plains, frequent dust storms and the

> There is a Kansas City in the northeast corner of Kansas and one in the northwest corner of Missouri. It is essentially the same city, simply divided by a state line and the Missouri and Kansas Rivers. The smaller of the two cities is in Kansas; it has a population of 149,767; a mayor (of the city and of Wyandotte County) who is also called the chief executive officer, or CEO; the National Football League's Chiefs; Major League Baseball's Royals; and Major League Soccer's Wizards.

impossibility of competing with large corporate farms have made agriculture a far less profitable endeavor than it once was.

Above the plains in the state seal are rolling hills and, above them, thirty-four stars representing Kansas's place in the United States' expanding family of states. Above the stars is the state motto, *"Ad Astra per Aspera,"* Latin for "To the Stars Through Difficulties." This would seem to be a tribute to the original settlers, who dreamed so grandly when they left their homes and moved westward.

Above the seal is the state crest, a sunflower above a bar of blue and gold. The sunflower is the state flower, and the blue and gold represent the Louisiana Purchase, which made the lands of Kansas a part of the United States. Colorado and North Dakota also use these colors to recognize their ties to the French. Beneath the state seal is "Kansas" in large, yellow block letters.

Lebanon, Kansas, is the town situated closest to the geographical center of the continental United States.

Kansas became the nation's thirty-fourth state on January 29, 1861. As a result of 1854's Kansas-Nebraska Act, which overturned the Missouri Compromise, Kansas did not have to enter the Union as a slave state or a free state. The people of the state were free to answer the slavery question on their own. This is called "self-determination"; Kansans could decide certain things (by voting on certain issues or by voting for certain representatives) for themselves. Self-determination is one of the ideas that enables a political philosophy like federalism to really work.

On April 12, 1861, two and a half months after Kansas joined the Union, the Civil War began. But Kansans had already been at war for years. After the passage of the Kansas-Nebraska Act, there was awful infighting as both proslavery forces and abolitionists flocked to the state. Both sides were determined to tip the balance of Congress in their favor. The term "Bleeding Kansas" aptly describes the tension and bloodshed of this period. After achieving statehood, Kansans voted in favor of slavery. However, Kansas remained on the side of the Union once the war began.

Sixty-six years after statehood, state legislators adopted a flag. The use of thin bands of white to separate colors allows the colors of a flag to stand out. In this, Kansas's flag scores a perfect ten. However, with its blue field and state seal, the flag is lacking in distinctiveness. Any flag that employs a state seal runs this risk. If a seal is used, the images should be clear both from five feet and fifty feet, on a large banner or a tiny lapel pin. This is why Kansas's flag was sixty-ninth out of seventy-two flags in the "Great NAVA Survey of 2001." Kansans must ask themselves if their flag is appropriate, both in terms of appearance and in terms of its symbols, given lingering questions of the design's historical accuracy. This could be an issue of self-determination if the people of the state don't like the answers.

There are actually two different time zones in Kansas. While most of the state is in the Central Time Zone, some of its western counties employ Mountain Time.

Oregon has its Beavers and Fighting Ducks, but the University of Kansas has its Jayhawks. This name originated during the troubled times of "Bleeding Kansas." The jayhawk is a fictitious bird, a combination of a blue jay and a hawk. Although the term was first used in a derogatory manner, it soon became a patriotic name for anyone who was antislavery. Lawrence, where the University of Kansas is located, was an antislavery city.

You can still hear UK students chanting, "Rock chalk, Jayhawk! KU!" at the school's sporting events. Limestone, also known as chalk rock, surrounds the school's campus.

West Virginia

West Virginia

Admitted
June 20, 1863

Before West Virginia could stand on its own, this mountainous land was a part of Virginia. Virginia, a state since 1788, had just decided to secede from the Union when representatives from western Virginia stormed out of the state's capitol building. This mutiny was symbolic of the turmoil that was gripping the nation. The year was 1861.

The Civil War was only days old when Virginia made its decision. Representatives from the state's western counties wished to remain part of the United States and a few months after the incident at the capitol building, the residents of thirty-nine counties voted in favor of statehood (the presence of Union soldiers kept most Confederate sympathizers away from the polls). Congress approved an Act of Admission after a somewhat hypocritical debate over whether or not to allow any form of slavery in the soon-to-be state, and President Lincoln issued a Presidential Proclamation on April 20, 1863. Sixty days later, on June 20, 1863, West Virginia became our thirty-fifth state.

Before the strife of the Civil War, there were other problems in West Virginia. In particular, there were numerous conflicts between the Native Americans and the colonists, including the French and Indian Wars, which lasted from 1754 to 1763. In the end, the British were victorious and the colonists were told to steer clear of this still-dangerous area. However, settlers returned to the land that would someday be West Virginia, and more fighting ensued. On October 10, 1774, Lord Dunmore's War, a succession of skirmishes between Virginia's militia and local Native Americans, came to an end and the land was thought to finally be safe for settlement.

The British had different plans, though, using this bad blood between the natives and the Virginians to their advantage during the Revolutionary War. The Native Americans who had been chased from the land fought alongside the Red Coats. Once the war was over, and the British and the Native Amer-

Three world-class athletes have called West Virginia home at one time or another: George Brett, a Hall of Fame third baseman for the Kansas City Royals; gold–medal winning Olympic gymnast Mary Lou Retton; and NBA icon Jerry West.

icans had been defeated, these problems disappeared for good. The colonists were now Americans, and this was their home.

On June 20, 1863, West Virginia was admitted to the Union, but not every resident was pleased to hear that it was entering as a free state. Although a clear majority had sought statehood, the split was almost fifty-fifty on the slave issue. One of West Virginia's sons stayed loyal to Virginia and to the South: General Thomas "Stonewall" Jackson would end up giving his life for the Confederacy.

The Civil War ended in 1865, and by 1872 African Americans were allowed to vote and hold public office in West Virginia. In 1873, the state adopted its official seal. The seal, also referred to as the coat of arms, pays tribute to West Virginia's industry, agriculture, and steadfast dedication to defending liberty. A seal committee, consisting of members of the state legislature, commissioned an artist named Joseph H. Diss Debar to create the art for the seal. The legislature accepted his design, and West Virginia had its first identifying mark. The seal has never been changed.

> **West Virginia, home of the Mountaineers, has an average altitude of 1,500 feet. No state east of the Mississippi stands taller.**

Most notable on the seal is a large boulder engraved with "June 20, 1863," the date of statehood. This boulder stands for strength. It also stands between two men, a miner and a farmer. Each has laid his rifle at his feet; the guns crisscross in the grass, signifying a position of peace until circumstances dictate otherwise. Resting on top of these rifles is a liberty cap, reinforcing the idea that West Virginians will fight to defend their freedom.

Each man is holding the tools of his trade. The farmer stands in front of a stalk of corn with his ax and his plow. The miner carries a pickax and stands in front of an anvil and sledgehammer.

Fifty-six years after adopting the seal, West Virginia placed it on a field of white to create its first flag. On March 7, 1929, Senate Joint Resolution Number 18 made the flag official. Like the state seal, this flag has gone unchanged over the years. The resolution outlines the flag's appearance in great detail: "The proportions of the flag of the State of West Virginia shall be the same as those of the United States ensign; the field shall be pure white, upon the

West Virginia is known for its natural beauty. Travel here and you will find excellent skiing, hiking, white water rafting, and camping. It is also a favorite destination of hunters and fishermen. There are even mineral springs, including Berkeley Springs and White Sulphur Springs. The Greenbrier, in White Sulphur Springs, is the state's most renowned resort; once used as a retreat for the president and other government officials, the Greenbrier lists nuclear bomb–proof bunkers among its amenities.

center of which shall be emblazoned in proper colors, the coat-of-arms of the State of West Virginia upon which appears the date of the admission of the State into the Union, also with the motto, 'Montani Semper Liberi' (Mountaineers Are Always Free). Above the coat-of-arms of the State of West Virginia there shall be a ribbon lettered, 'State of West Virginia,' and arranged appropriately around the lower part of the coat-of-arms of the State of West Virginia a wreath of Rhododendron maximum in proper colors. The field of pure white shall be bordered by a strip of blue on four sides."

The Rhododendron maximum is the state flower. The state motto, "Montani Semper Liberi," is closely associated with the nickname applied to the citizens of West Virginia: the "Mountaineers." This eventually became the nickname of the state's biggest university, the University of West Virginia.

Nevada

Admitted

October 31, 1864

Nevada became the thirty-sixth state on October 31, 1864. This desert land first came to the public's attention during the Gold Rush of 1849; many pioneers passed through on their way to California. In 1857, prospectors discovered a silver mine in Nevada, and industry boomed in the place that had once been nothing more than a way station for fortune-seekers. For years to come, people would flock to Nevada. These days, the silver flows from slot machines, as tourism and gambling have become the state's leading money-makers.

Nevada was named for the Sierra Nevada Mountains, which separate the state from its neighbor to the west, California. The area, which was a part of the Utah Territory between 1850 and 1864, attracted mainly Mormons and fox and beaver fur traders until news of the Comstock Lode spread. This silver mine made the land famous, and settlement began here in earnest; Congress even made Nevada a territory in March 1861. Although Nevada did not yet meet the population requirement for becoming a state, President Abraham Lincoln wanted it as a part of the Union so that he would have enough votes to pass the Thirteenth Amendment to the United States Constitution. This amendment, also known as the Emancipation Proclamation, was the official government decree that outlawed slavery in all Confederate states. Nevada joined the Union as a free state in October 1864.

Nevada raised its first flag in 1905. Silver and gold was the theme: "Nevada" was printed in gold in the center of the dark blue field and bracketed on each side by a silver star. At the top of the flag was the word "Gold," written in gold. At the bottom of the flag, "Silver" was written in silver. There

> Known for its entertainment, Las Vegas once played host to a record number of Elvis Presley shows. Elvis's "Vegas Years" began on July 31, 1969, when he took the stage at the newly-opened International Hotel. This was the first of 637 concerts! His last show was on December 12, 1976 (by that time the hotel had been renamed The Hilton), and Elvis impersonators have been trying to recapture the magic ever since.

also were thirty-six silver and gold stars on the flag, representing Nevada's position as the thirty-sixth state.

In 1915, Nevada designed a more tasteful, but no more subtle, flag. The stars were still included, in all their silver and gold glory, but they were now smaller and rearranged around the state seal. In 1926, Nevada Lieutenant Governor Maurice Sullivan decided Nevada needed a simpler, more economical state flag. How the state got that flag is a story in itself.

Lt. Governor Sullivan created a contest, offering a $25 prize to the resident who designed the best flag. Louis Shellback, a museum curator in Reno, won the contest. However, after the Republicans swept the 1926 Nevada elections, Mr. Shellback moved to New York, and he and his flag were temporarily forgotten. In 1929, Senator William Dressler brought up the issue again, and Mr. Shellback's design was brought before the State Senate. The senators discussed Senate Bill 51 at length, trying to determine whether or not to include the state's name on the flag. Finally, on March 26, 1929, the Senate presented the bill to Governor Balzar, who signed the flag specifications into law. There was just one problem: the agreed-upon placement of "Nevada" had been mistakenly omitted from the bill.

> In 1848, after the Mexican-American War, Mexico ceded to the United States the land that would become Nevada, along with California, Texas, Arizona, Utah, and parts of New Mexico and Colorado.

Nevada had its first official state flag, but the confusion would not be cleared up, incredibly enough, until 1991. That year the state legislature decided on the final placement of "Nevada," thus improving upon the original Shellback design. The flag has not changed since 1991.

Today Nevada's flag features a field of cobalt blue as well as two sprays of sagebrush, the state flower. The sagebrush stems cross at the bottom to form a half-wreath. Technically, the canton of the flag is the upper left corner, closest to the top of the flagpole. On Nevada's flag the sagebrush is in the canton, below one large, silver star. Above this star appear the words "Battle Born."

"Battle Born," officially adopted as the state slogan on March 26, 1937, refers to Nevada's having been the only state to achieve statehood during the

Nickname
"Silver State"

Motto
"All for Our Country"

> **The structural volume of Nevada's Hoover Dam is greater than even the largest pyramid in Egypt. On average, it took 100,000 men and twenty years to complete each pyramid. Five thousand workers labored for four years to build the Hoover Dam.**

Civil War. On the flag the slogan is scrolled in black on a golden-yellow banner. "Nevada" appears in the same golden color, between the silver star and the sagebrush stems; the sagebrush flowers are also golden-yellow. According to government decree, the state slogan is to be written in "black-colored sans serif gothic capital letters."

It may seem ironic that, in Spanish, *Nevada* means "snow covered." But the state of Nevada is not completely devoid of snow. There is wonderful skiing in the Lake Tahoe region. Much of Nevada's history is similarly surprising and fascinating. It is a history that includes changes in national allegiance (from Mexican to American), in territorial name (from the Utah Territory to the Nevada Territory), in wealth (from desert way station to source of silver and gold), and in statehood (from territory to state by Presidential Proclamation). It is a state that is changing and growing even now.

The 2000 census shows that the population of Nevada is 1,998,257 people. This is an incredible 66.3 percent increase since 1990! Nevada is, by far, America's fastest-growing state and has been for quite some time. Between 1950 and the 2000 census, the state's population grew by 1,200 percent.

Nebraska

Nebraska

Admitted

March 1, 1867

T he French fur traders were the first Europeans to settle in the area that would come to be known as Nebraska. After the Louisiana Purchase, American explorers Lewis and Clark passed through the area. And in the years to come, Nebraska would play host to the Oregon, California, and Mormon Trails, the Pony Express mail delivery service, and the Union Pacific Railroad. In using Nebraska as a byway, each played a role in bringing people, even if temporarily, to the area. Many of these pioneers ended up staying. Under the provisions of the Homestead Act of 1862, as long as these settlers farmed the land successfully, it was theirs for a minimal fee. The Homestead National Monument of America still stands in Nebraska today.

Kansas and Nebraska were both given territory status as the debate over slavery raged. People coming to Nebraska from the South brought slaves with them, and citizens of the territory voted to allow slavery when a slave was moved in from another state. Free men, however, could remain free. The Kansas-Nebraska Act put the onus of responsibility on local government, reversing the trend set by the Missouri Compromise, and in January of 1861, Nebraska's legislature passed, despite the governor's veto, an act to abolish slavery in the territory. This legislation, coupled with the end of the Civil War in 1865, and the Emancipation Proclamation, settled the question of slavery in Nebraska once and for all. One issue that was yet to be resolved here, however, was statehood.

Nebraska had applied for statehood in 1864, but Congress would not approve its petition due to a problem with the state constitution that Nebraska's leaders, including Governor David Butler, had composed. The problem lay in the restriction of voting to white males only. In order to gain state status this provision was dropped, by legislative vote, from the constitution, and on

The lowest temperature ever recorded in the state is minus 47 degrees Fahrenheit—twice. The first was at Camp Clarke, in 1899. Ninety years later the same temperature was recorded at Oshkosh.

March 1, 1867, Nebraska became our thirty-seventh state. The Nebraska state seal was designed in the same year and would end up being the basis for the state's official flag.

The focal point of the state seal is a blacksmith hammering on his anvil. Behind the blacksmith, representing the state's agricultural enterprises, are sheaves of wheat and stalks of corn. Nebraska was first known as the "Tree Planters' State," from 1895 to 1945, because Arbor Day has its roots in Nebraska. Since then Nebraska has followed the lead of the sports teams from the University of Nebraska and gone by the nickname the "Cornhuskers."

A settler's cabin, in the background of the seal, sits by the Missouri River. This is in tribute to the spirit of the pioneers who first settled the land. A steamboat plies the river, and beyond the river a westbound train heads toward the Rocky Mountains.

A flowing banner covers the sky in Nebraska's seal. Scrolled in gold is the state motto: "Equality before the Law." In a circle surrounding this seal is "Great Seal of the State of Nebraska" at the top and "March 1, 1867," the date of statehood, on the bottom.

Nebraska's elevation slopes gently upward from one side of the state to the other. From the fertile plateaus of the east to the first hints of the Rocky Mountains in the west, Nebraska slowly rises from 840 feet along the Missouri River to 5,424 feet in elevation.

It was not until 1925 that the state would fly its first flag, making it one of the last states to adopt an official "flag." As a matter of fact, until 1963, the state referred to its most important symbol as the "State Banner." In 1965, the state legislature made one final change to the statutes, outlining the manner in which the flag should be used. The flag of Nebraska is to fly at all events, and in all locations, where it is deemed appropriate to fly the United States flag (the state flag, as tradition dictates, flies beneath or to the left of "Old Glory").

When the topic of a flag first came up, Nebraska's legislators were fickle. They wanted the flag to be perfect. In 1921, they turned down a design submitted by an architect from New York. Four years later, though, the senators

Nickname
"Cornhusker State"

Motto
"Equality Before the Law"

Most states are presided over by a governor, a senate, and a house of representatives. This is not the case, however, in Nebraska. Employing a system called "unicameral legislation" (*uni* means "one"), Nebraska has only a governor and a senate. The state does not elect a house of representatives.

came to an agreement and this version of the flag, the state's first, still hangs in the office of the secretary of state of Nebraska. This office is in Lincoln, but Omaha was once the capital of the state. There is actually an incredible story behind the switch from Omaha to Lincoln.

State seals are often featured on a state's flag. Even if this was not the case in Nebraska, according to state law the seal has to be displayed in the state's capitol building. In 1868, there was a faction, including Nebraska's governor and secretary of state, that wanted to make Lincoln the capital city.

Governor Butler and Nebraska Secretary of State Thomas Kennard planned on slipping out of Omaha one night and sliding into Lincoln a few days later. As long as Secretary Kennard had the state seal with him, they could rightfully claim Lincoln to be the state's capital. Legend has it that Secretary Kennard removed the official seal from the capitol building, hid it under the seat of his buggy, and traveled to Lincoln, arriving the following Monday. Governor Butler met him there, and Lincoln has been the state capital ever since.

Colorado

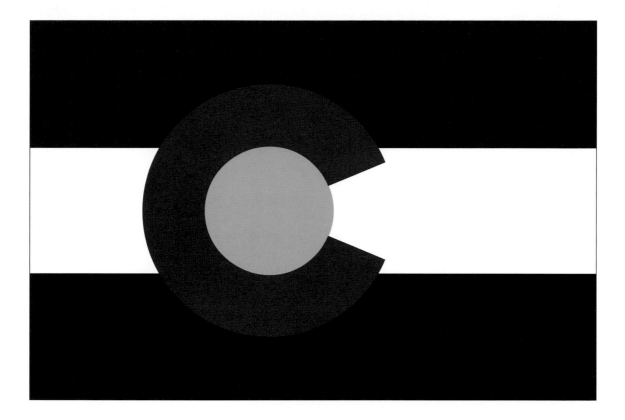

149

Colorado

Admitted

August 1, 1876

Colorado's petition for statehood was granted on August 1, 1876. If you look closely at the year in which President Ulysses S. Grant signed the Act of Admission, it is no surprise to learn that one of Colorado's nicknames is the "Centennial State": the United States was celebrating its one-hundredth anniversary in the year that it added the thirty-eighth state. The previous state to join the Union had been Nebraska, nine years earlier. The United States was growing at a decent pace, but not since the fifteen-year gap between Missouri and Arkansas had there been so much time between Acts of Admission. On average, a colony or territory had been granted statehood every two and a half years since 1776.

There was very little controversy surrounding Colorado's statehood. For example, the United States government was able to carve the state out from the land. It was Congress that determined the state's boundaries, making Colorado one of the few states to have not one of its borders determined by nature. Only Colorado, Wyoming, and North Dakota can claim to have a shape that so closely resembles a rectangle; all have the federal government to thank for this.

Colorado does have a major river running through it, but its location precludes it from serving as a boundary. The Colorado River is the biggest river of the American Southwest. It drains approximately 242,000 square miles of land in

> One stopover that many Americans make while touring the West is the "Four Corners," where Colorado, Arizona, New Mexico, and Utah meet. This is the only spot in the country where you can be in four different states at once.

Colorado, Wyoming, Utah, New Mexico, Arizona, Nevada, and California. Like with several other states, Colorado's name is derived from its main river. In Spanish, the word *colorado* means "colored red." When Spanish explorers first saw the Colorado River, the color of the rock formations around the river made the water appear red. "Colorful Colorado" is another of this state's nicknames.

Andrew Carlisle Johnson designed the original Colorado flag in 1911, and it is the only flag that Colorado has ever known. Whether you find its beauty to be aesthetic, social/ethical, or vexillogical, the flag of Colorado, with its four colors and simple, distinct appearance is handsome and easily recognizable. The most prominent feature is the letter "C," printed in red. The layout of the flag, as well as the "C" for Colorado, were standardized by the state's General Assembly in 1964.

On three sides, the letter "C" surrounds a perfect circle of gold. It is also outlined in the state statute that the flag should be accompanied by a cord of gold and silver intertwined with gold and silver tassels. This color choice might be a nod to Colorado's mining; in the early days of settlement, silver and gold were found there just as in Nevada and California. The red "C" is set on a field of three horizontal blue and white stripes, equally sized. This design earned Colorado's flag sixteenth place (out of seventy-two flags) in the "Great NAVA Survey of 2001."

Before February 28, 1929, there was confusion as to the exact colors of the flag. As the design, and reproduction, of flags became more of an exact science, Colorado's state legislature decided to outline the specifications of their most important symbol. So the General Assembly decided to simply make reference to "Old Glory," the official flag of our nation. These shades of red, white, and blue are meant to match those on the American flag.

Colorado has 4,301,261 citizens (according to the 2000 census), which makes it the twenty-fourth most-populous state in America. The number of U.S. Representatives as well as the number of electoral votes that a state has are linked to the population. Colorado has six representatives and eight electoral votes.

Nicknames

"Centennial State"
"Colorful Colorado"

Motto

"Nothing Without Providence"

Recently, construction workers from the Denver Paving Company discovered parts of a seven-ton Columbian mammoth. This creature is a distant cousin to the woolly mammoth. Although the creature's entire skeleton was not found, researchers from the Denver Museum of Natural History think that the animal could have been nearly twenty feet long and that it walked the earth approximately 50,000 years ago.

It is also said that the four colors of the flag relate back to Colorado's natural beauty. Since Colorado is known for its majestic mountains, white is used on the flag to represent snow. The blue is for the Colorado sky. The gold is for the sunshine that fills that sky every day. And the red represents the color of the soil. "Colorful Colorado" is definitely an appropriate nickname.

In 1964, the General Assembly again addressed the flag's specifications; no one knew for certain

> **Seventy-five percent of the land in the United States sitting at an altitude of 10,000 feet or higher is located in Colorado. Of all fifty states, Colorado has the highest mean altitude.**

what the size and location of the "C" was supposed to be. The General Assembly determined the following: the "circular red C" must be set one-fifth of the way across the flag, closer to hoist side (or "the staff end of the flag"), and "the diameter of the letter is two-thirds of the width of the flag." There would be no more debate; the law had been written and the specifications of the state flag were now set in stone. Other than the statutes put into effect in 1929 and 1964, the only flag that Colorado has ever known has flown free of controversy.

> **The official state dance of Colorado is the square dance. Interested citizens can even locate their local square dancing council on the Colorado State Square Dance Association website (http://www.squaredancing.com/colorado/).**

North Dakota

153

North Dakota

Admitted
November 2, 1889

North Dakota and South Dakota were the thirty-ninth and fortieth states accepted into the Union. They were signed into statehood on the same day: November 2, 1889. From 1861 to 1889, this part of the country had been known as the Dakota Territory. Along with the land that would become North and South Dakota, the territory included parts of Montana and Wyoming. To the Sioux Indians, *Dakota* means "friend." The Sioux tribe that was native to this area was known as the Dakota Sioux.

In the late 1800s, several factors led to the population growth in the Dakotas. The discovery of gold, the introduction of cattle ranching, the Dakota Sioux fleeing to Canada, and the new railroads all played a part in North Dakota and South Dakota asking to be recognized as separate states. In order to attain state status, a territory must present to the United States Congress its census numbers (a population of at least 60,000 people is required for statehood; North Dakota alone had just under 200,000 residents) and an agreeable state constitution. The Omnibus Bill of 1889 gave North and South Dakota, as well as Washington and Montana, the green light to construct their state constitutions.

One result of Manifest Destiny and the Monroe Doctrine (President James Monroe's effort to curb European intervention in the Western Hemisphere) was the United States' involvement in the Spanish-American War. Cuba was seeking independence from Spain at this time, and the United States was motivated to help by several factors, including Cuba's proximity to Florida. North Dakota's infantry fought in both the Spanish-American War in 1898 and the Philippine Island Insurrection in 1899. The flag these troops carried impressed Colonel John H. Fraine so much that on January 21, 1911, he presented a resolution (House Bill Number 152) to the state legislature to make this regi-

In 1947 and again in 1989, North Dakota's state legislature defeated bills that sought a name change for the state. The intention was to drop the word *North* from North Dakota, so that the state's name would simply be Dakota, as it once was.

mental flag the official flag of North Dakota. Colonel Fraine was also a state representative, so it only made sense for him to introduce this bill to the House.

The North Dakota flag has a particularly patriotic design. Rising above the state's name is a bald eagle. Protecting the bird's breast is a second tribute to the nation: the traditional shield consisting of a blue field and thirteen red and white stripes, a reference to the original thirteen states. In its right talon the eagle carries an olive branch of peace, and in its left talon are the arrows of war. In its beak the eagle holds a red ribbon with the words *"E Pluribus Unum,"* or "Out of many, one," stitched in gold. According to the secretary of state, though, the preferred interpretation in North Dakota is, "One nation made up of many states."

Thirteen gold stars in two rows twinkle above the eagle's head. The stars are situated beneath the golden rays of a rising sun, a tribute to the birth of the new nation. The design

Acquired as a part of the Louisiana Purchase, North Dakota is one of eleven states to share a border with Canada. The southern part of the state was ceded by Britain as a part of the Treaty of Ghent in 1818.

is set against a field of dark blue. When the legislators agreed to adopt this flag, on March 3, 1911, the only change they made was to add the state's name. It would appear on the bottom of the flag, white letters against a red background, contained within a golden scroll.

The state flag of North Dakota was adopted in 1911, the same year that Colorado adopted its state flag. And, as in Colorado, the appearance of North Dakota's flag has not changed since its inception. In 1953, a bill to alter the flag was presented and defeated before the state legislature. One argument for change was that the flag too closely resembles the coat of arms of the United States; another argument was the flag does not really represent the state. Aside from the name at the bottom of the flag, what is there in its design to teach us about North Dakota? Although patriotic images are always welcome, a more fitting flag might pay tribute to the state's rich agricultural history, its rolling fields of wheat, its wild prairie rose (the state flower), or perhaps its

Nicknames

"Peace Garden State"
"Flickertail State"
"Roughrider State"

Motto

"Liberty and Union, Now and Forever, One and Inseparable"

history of fur trade—although this is as unlikely as an image of the Native Americans who once lived in the Dakotas. Traders from the Hudson Bay, North West, and American Fur Companies virtually drained the area of buffalo and beaver. To re-

July is the warmest month of the year in North Dakota. Temperatures average between 67 and 73 degrees Fahrenheit.

member a time when two species of animal nearly became extinct might not be the best way to commemorate statehood!

When President Benjamin Harrison signed North and South Dakota into statehood, he did not look to see which document he put his pen to first. The president did not want to show favoritism. Therefore, we don't know which state was really the thirty-ninth, and which was the fortieth, to enter the Union. In the end, though, it didn't matter. Common sense prevailed as that age-old determiner of succession, alphabetical order, was used, making North Dakota the thirty-ninth state.

North Dakota's main source of income is agriculture. The majority of its farms raise cattle, wheat, and barley. The first people to farm the land here were the Mandan, Arikara, and Hidatsa tribes. Unfortunately, a majority of the Mandan could not survive a smallpox epidemic, introduced by European fur traders in 1837.

Today, there are five reservations in North Dakota. The Fort Berthold Reservation is home to the "Three Affiliated Tribes," the Arikara, the Hidatsa, and the Mandan.

South Dakota

South Dakota

Admitted
November 2, 1889

South Dakota is a land of incredible natural beauty and unique sites. In the southeastern part of the state are the Badlands, a broad expanse of incredible rock outcroppings. This national park looks like the dark side of Mars! The state also boasts the Black Hills in the southwest and the Great Plains in the west. Whether it stands for the golden corn above ground or the precious metal hidden below, gold is an appropriate color for South Dakota. When you consider that plus the blue sky that seems to stretch forever overhead, the colors of the state flag make sense.

On the flag's field of sky blue sits the picturesque state seal of South Dakota. The seal features a farmer plowing his field. This is a theme seen in many other states: pioneers moved out west; cleared the land and planted it; grew crops and made a living for themselves; and made a home for their families. They took the frontier land of the Wild West, settled it, and brought it all the way to statehood.

This particular farmer is tending a field of corn, with two horses pulling his plow. Below the field, on the Missouri River, a steamboat carries crops, fur, or perhaps even passengers upriver. Before the railways arrived here, the steamboat was a popular mode of transportation. The plume of steam coming from the boat floats skyward and runs parallel to a stream of smoke coming from the smokestack of a smelt furnace on the banks of the river. This smelt furnace represents the mining that takes places throughout South Dakota. It is gold that people found in the Black Hills, and it is gold people are still looking for today.

While one of the tenets of the United States is the separation of church and state, the country's history includes many examples of religion mixing with

Six of the *Little House on the Prairie* books are set in De Smet. Although Laura Ingalls Wilder eventually moved to Missouri with her husband, Almanzo, most of her family is buried here. The memory of this beloved author is preserved by the Laura Ingalls Wilder Memorial Society whose headquarters are in the very same town.

government. In this case, religion mixes with a government symbol. A gold banner cresting the upper curve of South Dakota's state seal reads, "Under God the People Rule." This sentiment, which is South Dakota's state motto, speaks to the democratic ideals that guide the country and the states. When the colonies broke away from Great Britain, the foundation was laid: the people would rule.

Surrounding the state seal's scene is a sky blue ring. In the top of the ring is "State of South Dakota," and at the bottom is "1889," the year of statehood. Flanking the year are the words "Great" and "Seal." On the state flag, twenty-four gold points, representing the sun, surround the seal. This design rests on a sky blue field (thus replacing the dark blue of the state seal). To give the state name more prominence, it is repeated in large gold letters above the sun design. Beneath the sun is the official state nickname, "The Mount Rushmore State."

Like several other states, South Dakota adopted its official seal before it even became a state. This seal was designed in 1885 and represents South Dakota's commerce, industry, and natural resources.

> **South Dakota is the nation's leader in honey production. Clear clover honey is produced in South Dakota and mixed with the darker honey of other states before being bottled for sale. The honeybee was named the state insect in 1978.**

Another picturesque representation that can be found in South Dakota is Mount Rushmore. South Dakota's nickname is a reference to the state's dramatic mountain sculpture, as it was envisioned by John Gutzon de la Mothe Borglum. In 1923, Borglum was contacted by Doane Robinson, the superintendent of the South Dakota State Historical Society, to lead this patriotic project. Robinson was impressed by Borglum's credentials, which included laying the groundwork for the Confederate sculpture at Stone Mountain in Georgia. Borglum was hired, despite his failure to complete the Stone Mountain project and news of his affiliation with the Ku Klux Klan while in Georgia, and he worked on Mount Rushmore for fourteen years, right up until his death in 1941.

Mount Rushmore National Park draws thousands of people each year. They come to see this massive tribute to four of the country's most popular presidents: George Washington, Thomas Jefferson, Abraham Lincoln, and Teddy Roosevelt. As visitors approach the viewing area, they can see flags from all fifty states flying overhead.

In the mid-1800s, it was gold that brought people to the land that would someday be called South Dakota. Growth slowed after the Gold Rush, but the continued construction of transcontinental railways led to the great Dakota land boom from 1878 to 1886. The territory's population tripled, giving citizens even more reason for petitioning to attain state status. During the 1888 election, local Republicans used the calls for statehood as a campaign issue and won on that platform. Within a year, South Dakota would be a state and the city of Pierre would be South Dakota's capital.

It had been nine years between the granting of statehood for Nebraska in 1867 and Colorado in 1876, and then another thirteen years between Colorado's acceptance and the Acts of Admission for South Dakota, North Dakota, Washington, and Montana. In just one year, though, the United States had grown from thirty-eight to forty-two states.

> **Even though the state seal is handsome, South Dakota's flag finished sixty-eighth in the "Great NAVA Survey of 2001." Only Kansas, Montana, Nebraska, and Georgia fared worse.**

> **South Dakota's population grew significantly between the censuses of 1990 and 2000. While North Dakota's increased by .5 percent, South Dakota experienced an 8.5 percent increase. This brought its population to 754,844 people, making South Dakota the fifth-smallest state in the Union. North Dakota is the fourth-smallest.**

Montana

161

Montana shares a common history with many other Southern and Midwestern states in that it was once controlled by the French, then ceded to the Spanish for a time, was then reclaimed by the French, and finally was sold to the United States as part of the Louisiana Purchase. It was the Spanish who named Montana. *Montaña* means "mountainous" or "mountain land" in Spanish; the root of the word is found in the Latin *montaanus*, which also means "mountainous." Montana's highest point is Granite Peak, which stands at 12,799 feet.

In 1864, an act of the United States Congress separated the Montana Territory from the Idaho Territory. Twenty-five years later, on November 8, 1889, the United States Congress granted Montana its statehood. In just over one hundred years, the nation had gone from twelve states to forty-one states.

The history of the state's flag starts on February 9, 1865. One year after Montana was named a territory, Governor Sidney Edgerton signed an official territorial seal into law. Designer Francis M. Thompson must have been influenced by other state seals as he created a picturesque setting to capture the land and the people who worked that land. One of the dreams that drew Americans out West was striking it rich with gold and silver. With the California Gold Rush and the mining in Nevada, pioneers had good reason to leave their homes behind. Some of those who would end up calling Montana home came for the very same reason. Thus, the Spanish phrase *"Oro y Plata,"* or "Gold and Silver," that appears on the state seal in blue lettering, set against a white banner.

Montana's population is the seventh-smallest in the Union. According to the 2000 census, the population is only 902,195. Montana has yet to pass the one million mark, despite a 12.9 percent increase in population since the 1990 census. No one seems to be worrying about overcrowding in "Big Sky" country; even if the population continues to grow at this rate, Montana ranks fourth in the nation in total land area (147,046 square miles).

Behind this banner is a natural scene of grassy plains banked against the shores of the Missouri River. The river flows from the Great Falls of the Missouri River, bracketed by the Rocky Mountains. Beyond the waterfall is a rising sun set against a bright sky. In the foreground, sitting atop the grassy plains, are the tools of the state's trades: a farmer's plow and a miner's shovel and pickax. Although the territorial seal was first designed in 1865, it did not become the official state seal of Montana until Governor J. E. Rickards signed it into law on March 2, 1893.

By 1898, "Old Glory" was a forty-five-star flag. The First Territorial Infantry of Montana flew this flag as they trained to go into combat in the Spanish-American War. Units from all across Montana had gathered at Fort William Henry Harrison, just outside of Helena, in the spring of that year. These volunteers were training under Colonel Harry C. Kessler. Although the troops had a United States flag to fly as their regimental colors, Colonel Kessler felt that his men should have a special flag—something more representative of their homeland to be carried into battle. A group of women from Helena had bestowed upon them "Old Glory," and Colonel Kessler commissioned one of them to sew the state's seal onto a field of dark blue.

The First Territorial Infantry of Montana left to fight in the Philippine Insurrection in the fall of 1898. By the time they returned home one year later, their flag had been made famous in Montana's newspapers. Colonel Kessler presented the flag to the state's governor, Robert Smith. The Ninth Legislative Assembly of Montana was so taken with the image of the state seal on a field of blue that they voted in 1905 to make it the official state flag. The marking "1st Montana Infantry U.S.V." was dropped from the flag, and the only other change, committed to law in 1981, was the addition of the state's name, in

> As in California, the grizzly bear holds a special place in the hearts of the people of Montana. Named the official state mammal by a vote of schoolchildren in 1982, the grizzly is now a protected species. Animals close to becoming extinct may become protected by an act of the federal government.

Nickname
"Treasure State"

Motto
"Gold and Silver"

Montana's Glacier National Park features ice blue lakes and snow-capped mountains. As a matter of fact, if you are hiking up to one of the mountain-side chalets, chances are pretty good that you will be hiking through snow—even in July! The park, which opened in 1910, is also the world's first international park; it has a cooperative relationship with Canada's Waterton Lakes Park, and together they form Waterton-Glacier International Peace Park.

bright yellow, capital letters. "Montana" was placed at the top of the flag because State Representative Mel Williams and his wife, Eugenia, felt that the flag looked too similar to the flags of a number of other states. Montana's secretary of state, Jim Waltermire, took advantage of the pending legislation to outline the flag's exact specifications. In 1985, the lettering for the state name was changed to the font Helvetica bold. Other than that, the state flag has remained unchanged over the years, as has much of Montana.

The 1981 flag, with its Roman letters, along with the original flag of Montana, sewn by one of the women of Helena, and the first sketches of the state seal, drawn by Francis M. Thompson in 1865, are a part of the permanent collection of the Montana Historical Society. Appropriately enough, the Montana Historical Society is located in Helena.

Washington

165

Admitted

November 11, 1889

T he Washington Territory, established in 1853, was named for the country's first president, George Washington. When the state adopted a flag seventy years later, in 1923, it was only natural to include President Washington. The flag's design is simply the state seal, which already included a portrait of Washington, placed on a field of green. Washington's is the only green flag among the fifty state flags and the only one to include the image of an actual person.

Washington became the forty-second state on November 11, 1889, just three days after Montana was admitted to the Union. President Benjamin Harrison had a busy year: earlier in November, South and North Dakota had also attained state status. The country was growing, but after Washington only eight more states would be added.

Washington owes its official state seal to the Talcott brothers. In late 1889, the Washington legislature asked Charles Talcott, a jeweler, to design a seal. And fast. The legislature needed it in time for their November meeting. A committee had already started work on a design, which Talcott deemed far too complicated. The prospective seal was a crowded image of the port of Tacoma, wheat fields, sheep, and Mount Rainier. Talcott quickly reached for an ink bottle. He drew a circle around the bottle's base, placed a silver dollar inside the circle, and drew a second circle. Between the two rings he wrote, "The Seal of the State of Washington" and "1889." In the center of this double circle, he pasted a postage stamp that featured the bust of our first president and Revolutionary War hero, George Washington. The legislature quickly accepted the design.

Puget Sound extends inland from the Pacific Ocean, making both Olympia and Seattle port cities. Environmentalists are making the effort to protect this waterway. According to its website, one non-profit group, the People for Puget Sound, is "working to protect and restore the health of Puget Sound and the Northwest Straits through education and action. Our vision is a clean and healthy Sound, teeming with fish and wildlife, cared for by people who live here."

But turning the postage stamp into a viable image was no easy task. When magnified, the picture became blurred. As Flagman reminded us in the Introduction, an image needs to be distinguishable on a flag from fifty feet away or on a lapel pin. Talcott's brother, George, was given the job of finding a suitable image and cutting the printing die (the mold that would be used to reproduce this image). He finally found what they were looking for: a drawing of George Washington on a box of medicine, "Dr. D. Jaynes Cure for Coughs & Colds." Another Talcott brother, Grant, did the lettering, and Washington had its seal.

Over the years, a number of versions of the Talcott design were used, so in 1967, upon the request of the secretary of state, the General Assembly commissioned Seattle artist Richard Nelms to create a new insignia. Nelms selected a portrait of George Washington done by Gilbert Stuart and added it to the original Talcott layout. Washington's secretary of state, the custodian of both the state seal and flag, still has the original Talcott die and press, now more than one hundred years old.

The official state song, "Washington, My Home," was adopted in 1959. It was written by Helen Davis and arranged by Stuart Churchill. The closing lyrics are as follows: "We'll happy ever be/As people always free/For you and me a destiny/Washington my home/For you and me a destiny/Washington my home."

The flag's color specifications are taken from the Pantone Formula Guide. Pantone's colors are used for most of the flags produced in the United States and around the world. The background of Washington's flag is Irish Green (Pantone PMS 348); the background of the state seal is Oriental Blue (PMS 311); the portrait, letter, and inner rings of the state seal are black; George Washington's face is Flesh Tint (PMS 169); and the gold used in the state seal and fringe is Nugget Gold (PMS 116).

Washington did not adopt its flag until 1923, more than thirty years after the state was admitted to the Union. Before this, at the turn of the twentieth century, a military flag bearing a gold profile of President Washington on blue bunting flew throughout the state. Another design, closely related to the one

Nickname

"Evergreen State"

Motto

"Bye and Bye"

In 2002, the Washington legislature passed a law requiring that the flag of National League of POW/MIA Families, commemorating missing Vietnam veterans, be flown with the state and national flags on the following days: Armed Forces Day, Memorial Day, Flag Day, Independence Day, National POW/MIA Recognition Day (the third Friday of September), and Veteran's Day. The POW/MIA flag should fly beneath the flags of the United States and Washington.

Of the 1,908 American soldiers who fought in Vietnam and are listed as missing in action or unaccounted for, forty-seven are from Washington.

still in use today, featured a gold state seal centered on a purple or green background. A similar ceremonial banner is displayed in the State Reception Room of the Legislative Building in Olympia. When the legislature approved the state statute describing the design of the official state flag, it stipulated that the flag "shall be of dark green silk or bunting, bearing in its center a reproduction of the seal of the state of Washington." The original law allowed that green fringe could be used on the flag; two years later, the legislature changed the fringe color to gold. It would seem that Washington's flag has finally been perfected and standardized.

Idaho

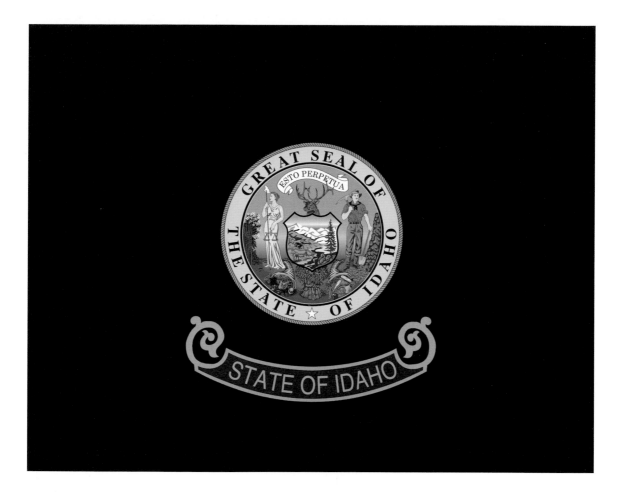

Admitted

July 3, 1890

On March 4, 1863, President Abraham Lincoln signed the act that established the Idaho Territory. The name *Idaho* has quite a story behind it. It was a mining lobbyist, George M. Willing, who coined the phrase *E Dah Hoe.* He was all too willing to tell people that this was a Native American phrase that meant "gem of the mountains." Even though members of the United States Senate quickly discovered that *Idaho* was a made-up word, they signed a bill to create the Idaho Territory. At that point, there was already a steamship on the Columbia River with the name in question, and when gold had been discovered on the Clearwater and Salmon Rivers, the mines were named the "Idaho Mines." What was done was done.

Before statehood was possible, the United States government had to secure the Idaho Territory and make the land safe for settlers. Without a population of 60,000, the transition from territory to state could not happen and in order to make the land safe for settlers, the Native American situation had to be resolved. Battles ensued, and as the United States defeated each successive tribe, it created another reservation. With very little land left, the United States could no longer chase the defeated tribes westward; land would have to be set aside within Idaho. President Ulysses S. Grant created the Coeur d'Alene Indian Reservation for the Coeur d'Alene and Spokane tribes in 1873; two years later he created the Lemhi Indian Reservation, for the Shoshonis, Bannocks, and Tukuarikas. In 1877, President Rutherford B. Hayes set aside the Duck Valley Indian Reservation, also in Idaho, for the Shoshonis and Paiutes.

Statehood came to Idaho, the forty-third state, on July 3, 1890. No official record remains of the first state seal, which had been adopted when Idaho was named a territory in 1863. Supposedly Silas D. Cochran, a clerk in the secre-

Adopted in 1967, the state gem of Idaho is the star garnet. This gem is usually dark purple in color and is considered to be more valuable than a ruby. Although *Idaho* does not actually translate to the "gem of the mountains," the Idaho star garnet is a true gem.

tary of state's office, designed a seal, but the territory's governor, Caleb Lyon, was not satisfied with it. He presented a seal of his own to the Idaho Territorial Legislature on January 11, 1866, and although not everyone approved, the territory used this seal until it became a state. With statehood came an official seal, designed by Emma Edwards Green, the first and only woman to design a state seal. When she submitted her design, Mrs. Green used her initials, because she feared rejections based on her gender. Idaho adopted the seal on March 14, 1891.

Mrs. Green, the daughter of a former governor of Missouri, won a competition sponsored by the First Legislature of the State of Idaho after spending a year at a New York art school. In her own words, Mrs. Green described the thought that went into the seal: "The question of Woman Suffrage was being agitated somewhat, and as leading men and politicians agreed that Idaho would eventually give women the right to vote, and as mining was the chief industry, and the mining man the largest financial factor of the state at that time, I made the

> There are more than two thousand lakes in Idaho but only 880 square miles of water. Lake Pend Oreille, at 180 square miles, is the state's largest lake.

figure of the man the most prominent in the design, while that of the woman, signifying justice, as noted by the scales; liberty, as denoted by the liberty cap on the end of the spear, and equality with man as denoted by her position at his side, also signifies freedom. The pick and shovel held by the miner, and the ledge of rock beside which he stands, as well as the pieces of ore scattered about his feet, all indicate the chief occupation of the State." This description, as seen on Idaho's state website, continued, "I was careful to make a thorough study of the resources and future possibilities of the State." As in the case of Washington's design, it is important that a state's seal and its flag symbolize the state as it is now, and as it will be, not as it was.

Mrs. Green's design incorporates many symbols. At the center of the seal is a shield, located between Justice and the miner. The tree in the foreground of the shield refers to Idaho's forests. The river is the Snake, or Shoshone, River. The man plowing, the sheaf of grain, the cornucopias, and the white represent Idaho's agricultural history. There is an elk's head above the shield and the state flower, the wild syringa, grows at Justice's feet.

As the turn of the century approached, Idaho still had no flag. The First Idaho Infantry, fighting in the Philippines in 1899 during the Spanish- American War, followed the lead of Montana's Colonel Kessler, flying the state seal on a field of blue. When Idaho's state legislature considered adopting an official flag, the suggestion was made to add "State of Idaho" to the infantry's design. So a golden scroll was included, twenty-one inches in diameter and two inches high, with the words "State of Idaho." The gold lettering, on a field of red, appears near the bottom of the flag. Idaho adopted its official state flag on March 12, 1907.

Fifty years later, Idahoan legislators authorized the standardization and improvement of the state seal, and flag, in order to more clearly highlight Idaho's

> It was in Idaho that the first Jewish governor was elected. For four years, between 1915 and 1919, Moses Alexander held that office.

industries (mining, agriculture, and forestry) and natural beauty. Artist Paul B. Evans was commissioned to paint this update of the original design; his work is now considered the official seal of Idaho. However, it is important to remember that during the early years of the feminist struggle, it was a woman who created Idaho's first official seal.

Wyoming

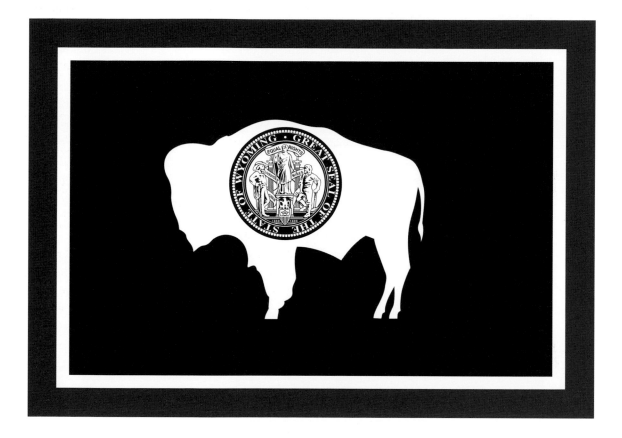

Wyoming

Admitted

July 10, 1890

As the nineteenth century drew to a close, the women's rights movement, concerned mainly with suffrage (or the right to vote), was gaining momentum. It was at this time that Wyoming earned its nickname, the "Equality State," and its motto, "Equal Rights." On December 10, 1869, Wyoming Territory Governor John A. Campbell signed into law a historic bill granting women the right to vote. The territorial government also gave women the right to hold public office; it was the first modern government in the world to grant such privileges.

Although many of the territory's legislators probably had the best interest of women in mind, there is no doubt that they were also thinking of statehood. If Wyoming was to attain state status, its population had to quadruple, and with the passing of this legislation leaders hoped to attract more families to the territory. The idea of women having the right to vote created a stir in Congress. As they considered Wyoming's statehood, many of the congressmen questioned the ability of women to vote wisely. Regardless, Wyoming was a trendsetter and by 1920 women's suffrage was made legal nationwide with the passing of the Nineteenth Amendment.

Wyoming finally achieved statehood on July 10, 1890, making it the forty-fourth of the United States. On January 31, 1917, the 14th State Legislature adopted the first official flag of Wyoming. The flag, designed by Verna Keays Keyes, features the state seal, which the 2nd State Legislature adopted in 1893. The seal includes two important dates: "1869," the year of Wyoming's first territorial government, and "1890," the date of statehood. The dates stand on either side of a red, white, and blue shield. Inside the shield is a

Wyoming is a Delaware Indian word meaning "upon the great plain." James M. Ashley, a congressman from Ohio, was the first to suggest the name. He had grown up in Pennsylvania, near the Wyoming Valley, and felt that this word would be perfect. The United States Congress applied it to the territory, which was created after the Dakota Territory was divided.

white five-pointed star stamped with "XLIV" (Roman numerals for forty-four), commemorating Wyoming's place as our nation's forty-fourth state.

In 1960, Mrs. Keyes described the meaning behind her flag. "The Great Seal of the State of Wyoming is the heart of the flag. The seal on the bison represents the truly western custom of branding. The bison was once 'Monarch of the Plains.' The red border represents the Red Men, who knew and loved our country long before any of us were here; also, the blood of the pioneers who gave their lives in reclaiming the soil. White is an emblem of purity and uprightness over Wyoming. Blue, which is found in the bluest blue of Wyoming skies and the distant mountains, has through the ages been symbolic of fidelity, justice and virility. And finally the red, white and blue of the flag of the State of Wyoming are the colors of the greatest flag in all the world, the Stars and Stripes of the United States of America."

> **The largest coal resources in America are in Wyoming. An estimated 1.4 trillion tons of coal can be found there. Wyoming leads the nation in the production of coal, bentonite, and trona.**

Most prominent on the seal is a woman, a direct reference to Wyoming's quest for equality. She stands on a pedestal, holding a banner that displays the words "Equal Rights." The men to her left and right represent Wyoming's cowboys and miners. The figures stand before two pillars; on top of each pillar is the Light of Knowledge. White scrolls wrapping around each pillar display the words "Oil," "Mines," "Livestock," and "Grain," Wyoming's four major industries.

Many states use their official seal in their flag design. But in placing its seal on the silhouette of a bison, Wyoming's flag distinguishes itself from all others. The flag also uses borders of red and white to differentiate itself from the state flags that feature a plain blue field. This unique design earned Wyoming's flag a spot in the top third of the "Great NAVA Survey of 2001"; it placed twenty-third out of seventy-two flags.

The cowboy on Wyoming's state flag has special significance. The oldest and largest outdoor rodeo in the world has taken place in Wyoming every year since 1897. And just about every night of the year there is a rodeo going on somewhere in the state. This is why, in addition to the "Equality State," Wyoming is known as the "Cowboy State." Probably the state's most recognizable symbol is the "Bucking Horse & Rider." This silhouette of a cowboy, hat held high as the horse tries to buck him, is actually trademarked. The image first appeared on state license plates in

> **Wyoming's state reptile is the horned toad— a lizard that resembles a toad, but with horny spines protruding from its head and body. The horned toad repels predators by squirting jets of blood from its eyes.**

1936 and is associated with the University of Wyoming, but the state's first use of the "Bucking Horse & Rider" dates back to before 1918. It was an insignia worn by Wyoming troops during World War I and was officially adopted by the United States Army as a means of identifying gun trails, trucks, helmets, and other equipment. Wyoming troops used the insignia in Korea and Vietnam and the symbol remains a source of pride.

> **A number of nations have flown their flags over the land that is now Wyoming. These include France, Great Britain, Mexico, Spain, and the United States. Several territorial flags have also flown over Wyoming, including those of the Dakotas, Idaho, Louisiana, Missouri, Nebraska, Oregon, Utah, and Washington territories.**

Utah

Utah

Admitted

January 4, 1896

The Spanish were the first Europeans to explore the territory that would come to be called Utah. But before the arrival of the Spanish explorers, and the subsequent settlement by American pioneers, the Native American tribes living in Utah included the Southern Paiute, Navajo, Gosiute, Northern, Eastern Shoshone, and the Ute. The state of Utah is named after the Ute. The Ute once called Utah and western Colorado home, but they were removed to reservations many years ago.

In July of 1847, Mormon pioneers entered the Salt Lake Valley. They were fleeing the persecution of the Midwest where their leader, Joseph Smith, and his brother had been assassinated. Like Roger Williams in Rhode Island, the Mormons sought religious freedom and a place where they would be able to govern themselves. In the Treaty of Guadalupe Hidalgo, signed on February 2, 1848, Mexico ceded a large parcel of land to the United States, including the land settled by the Mormons.

After the Mexican-American War ended, the Mormons were freed from Mexican rule and began to petition for statehood. However, the required Act of Admission would not be signed until 1896. For most of the 1800s, federally appointed governors (most of whom were not Mormon) made all decisions. During this time, followers of the religion made up 90 percent of the population; the remaining 10 percent who were not feared Mormon dominance and problems ensued. One point of disagreement was polygamy (which meant that Mormon men could have more than one wife).

> **Zion and Bryce Canyon National Parks are just two of Utah's natural highlights. With southern Utah's deep canyons, breathtaking views, and hikes for novices and pros, it is no wonder that people say all of the region could be a national park!**

Brigham Young, the leader of the Church of Jesus Christ of Latter-day Saints (members are called Mormons) and first governor of the Utah Territory, passed away in 1877. Within two decades, Utah would be able to settle its internal problems and finally hold a Constitutional Convention (1895), which resulted in statehood. One fact that worked in Utah's favor was that between 1860 and 1890 the territory's population jumped from 40,000 to more than

200,000. (The minimum population for state status was 60,000.) During this time, the Mormons established approximately five hundred towns in Utah and the surrounding states. Also of significance was a statement released to the Associated Press on September 25, 1890 by Mormon leader Wilford Woodruff: "I now publicly declare that my advice to the Latter-day Saints is to refrain from contracting any marriage forbidden by the law of the land." Polygamy would never again be a tenet of the Mormon faith. This declaration contributed to Congress's willingness to finally write an Act of Admission. Utah became a state on January 4, 1896, when President Grover Cleveland signed on the dotted line.

> **A recent highlight for America, as well as the people of Utah, was the 2002 Winter Olympics. This event was held in Salt Lake City and surrounding areas.**

On April 3 of that year, the state legislature approved an official seal for Utah. In the middle of this seal is a shield, and on top of the shield, with its wings spread wide, sits a bald eagle. Six arrows, three on each side, protrude from the shield. Beneath these arrows is the word "Industry," a tribute to the commerce of Utah. A beehive occupies the center of the shield, another symbol of commerce and of hard work. Surrounding the beehive are sego lilies, the official flower of Utah and a symbol of peace. The bulbs of the sego lily are actually edible, and legend has it that they saved the life of many a starving pioneer in the early years of settlement in Utah.

At the bottom of the shield is "1847," the year Mormons first settled in the region. Behind the shield are two American flags. Golden flagpoles are

> **Brigham Young's first attempt at statehood was called Deseret. This proposed state encompassed Utah, most of Nevada and Arizona, and parts of California, Wyoming, Colorado, New Mexico, Oregon, and Idaho. A constitution was even completed and sent to Washington, D.C., but the United States Congress refused to recognize Deseret as a state. Nevertheless, Brigham Young was elected governor of the territory in 1850.**

Nickname
"Beehive State"

Motto
"Industry"

visible, crisscrossed behind the shield, as are the red and white stripes, the blue field, and the white stars. Between two circular borders of gold braiding are the words "The Great Seal of the State of Utah." At the bottom is "1896" to commemorate the year Utah was finally granted statehood.

> In recent years, Utah's average age has been calculated at 27.1 years, making it the youngest of the fifty states.

As in many states, Utah's flag is simply the state seal placed on a field of blue. The official state flag, as we know it today, was designed in 1912 for the battleship USS *Utah*. One year later, Governor William Spry signed House Joint Resolution I and made this flag the official flag of Utah.

Utah's Mormon presence is still tremendous (approximately 70 percent of the population), making it a state like no other state. The church owns Zion Cooperative Mercantile Institute, the biggest department store in Salt Lake City, along with many other businesses around the state. The Mormons also publish *The Deseret*, one of Utah's best-selling newspapers.

> **The Church of Jesus Christ of Latter-day Saints differs from other religions in a number of ways. For example, Mormons study the *Book of Mormon*, which was published by Joseph Smith in 1830. They also believe that ancestors of the Native Americans, known as the Lamanites, were able to outlive their light-skinned counterparts, the Nephites.**

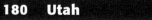

Oklahoma

More than fifty Native American tribes have called Oklahoma home. In addition, eight different "national" flags have flown over Oklahoma. In succession, they were the flags of Spain, Great Britain, France, Spain again, France again, the United States (after the Louisiana Purchase), Mexico, the Republic of Texas (before the Mexican-American War), the flag of the Choctaw tribe (for quite some time, the only Native American tribe to have a flag), and the Confederate flag, which was flown by Confederate sympathizers.

It was on November 16, 1907, that Oklahoma became the forty-sixth state to join the United States. Four years later, the state legislature approved Oklahoma's first official flag. The image was simple: a five-pointed star, outlined in blue and centered on a field of red, imprinted with the number forty-six.

After the Russian Revolution in 1917, Oklahomans complained that their state flag resembled the colors and symbols of Communism. The Daughters of the American Revolution held a flag contest, and Louise Funk Fluke, an artist from Oklahoma City, submitted the winning entry. In a tribute to the tribes that were native to or had been relocated to Oklahoma, the design combined Native American symbols with an olive branch on a field of sky blue. Mrs. Fluke chose this blue because the Choctaw flew a flag of the same color during the Civil War, when they battled against Confederate soldiers. The most engaging aspect of Oklahoma's flag is an Osage war shield centered just above the state name. The shield is the tanned hide of a buck or bison, decorated with six small white crosses; these crosses are actually Native American stars and represent high ideals. Seven eagle feathers hang from the lower half of the

The Oklahoma Dust Bowl was a natural disaster that contributed to the Great Depression of the 1930s. Farmers could not grow crops because of the lack of rain, and many lost their farms. These "Okies" were forced to leave their land and went to California in search of work. This low point in American history was immortalized in John Steinbeck's *The Grapes of Wrath.*

shield, and a calumet, or Native American peace pipe, is placed on top of the war shield. At one end of the peace pipe is the pipestone bowl; at the other is a tassel. Resting on top of the pipe is the ultimate American symbol of peace, the olive branch. It is significant that the peace pipe and olive branch are placed on top of the war shield.

Although the history of this country's Native Americans and settlers is anything but peaceful, there is a sense of balance in Oklahoma. The state has the largest Native American population of any state in the nation: almost 300,000 people of Native American ancestry call our forty-sixth state home. However, many of these tribes are not originally from Oklahoma. The infamous American policy of Indian Removal, initiated by President Andrew Jackson, is most often characterized by the Trail of Tears. This is the name that was given to the route of those thousands of Native Americans who were forced to leave their homes and move to reservation lands. This trail ended in Oklahoma. After Congress signed the Indian Removal Act into law in 1830, more than 15,000 Native Americans (including the "Five Civilized Tribes," the Cherokee, Choctaw, Creek, Chickasaw, and Seminole) were forced to migrate west. Not everyone agreed with the policy. In fact, Davy Crockett, then a congressman from Tennessee, saw his political career ruined when he spoke out against it. Between 1828 and 1845, these Southern tribes were forced to actually walk to Oklahoma. More than 4,000 died. The Osage, Kiowa, Comanche, and Apache already called Oklahoma home when the survivors from these other tribes arrived.

It is only fitting that the main symbols on Oklahoma's flag be Native American. What's more, the name *Oklahoma* comes from two Choctaw words, later combined by a missionary named Allen Wright. *Ukla* means "person," and *huma* means "red." The word first appeared in a Choctaw treaty in 1886. The state's name, scrolled in bold white letters across the bottom of the flag, was added in 1941. A minority of the legislators were convinced that this was

The western part of the state is referred to as the Oklahoma Panhandle. Extending in a thin strip above Texas, this stretch of land looks like the handle, while the rest of the state looks like the pan.

Nickname
"Sooner State"

Motto
"Labor Conquers All Things"

Oklahoma's nickname is the "Sooner State." In 1889, the federal government opened the Indian Territory up to pioneers, and thousands came to claim land. They lined up at the border until the signal "Start claiming!" was given, but some sneaked ahead to get the best land. These cheaters became known as "Sooners," because they started claiming land sooner than everyone else.

not necessary because they, along with a number of citizens, felt that the flag already distinguished itself with its unique design. The lesson is this: just because democracy rules does not mean that good taste prevails. Oklahoma's flag was ranked thirty-ninth out of seventy-two flags in the "Great NAVA Survey of 2001" and surely would have scored higher had the state's name never been included.

Oklahoma's state seal, although it does not appear on the flag, is also a tribute to the state's diversity. A white star appears in the center of a gold and blue circle. In each of the star's five points are symbolic representations of each of the "Five Civilized Tribes." Forty-five small golden stars surround this star, representing the forty-five states that made up the Union at the time that Oklahoma attained statehood on November 16, 1907. The large star, with its images at each of the five points, is the seal's forty-sixth star. It represents the state of Oklahoma. Although the seal is both handsome and symbolic, it was wise not to make it the focal point of the state flag. Mrs. Fluke's design seems to say more with less.

New Mexico

185

New Mexico

Admitted

January 6, 1912

Five years after Oklahoma became a part of the United States, its neighbor to the west, New Mexico, was recognized in an Act of Admission on January 6, 1912, and became the forty-seventh state to join the Union.

Nearly 42.1 percent of New Mexico's population today qualifies as Hispanic, which is reflective of the state's roots (9.5 percent of the population is Native American, and 66.8 percent is white; the percentages exceed 100 because of mixed heritage). It is no surprise to learn that explorers from New Spain (Mexico) named this land during the sixteenth century. The state song, "Así Es Nuevo Méjico," or "Thus Is New Mexico," is sung in both Spanish and English. The flags of Spain, Mexico, the Confederate States of America, and the United States have all flown over New Mexico during its long history.

In 1920, the New Mexico Chapter of the Daughters of the American Revolution began to push for a flag to replace the original state flag, which had been authorized in 1915. The original flag, designed by New Mexico historian Ralph Emerson Twitchell, featured an American flag in the upper left canton and the state seal in the lower right. "New Mexico" was stitched in a diagonal line from the lower left canton to the upper right. The DAR felt New Mexico deserved a flag that was more representative of the state's history and character. They finally gained permission to hold a flag contest in 1923, and Dr. Harry Mera, a physician and archeologist from Santa Fe, submitted the winning design which was sewn by his wife, Reba. In March 1925, Governor Arthur T. Hannett signed the Mera design into law. New Mexico finally had its new official state flag. This flag has not changed since.

> **With 1,819,046 citizens recorded during the 2000 census, New Mexico is ranked thirty-sixth in the country in population. This number may seem low, but it is an increase of 20.1 percent since 1990. There is room to grow, though. New Mexico is the fifth-largest state in the Union at 121,666 square miles; this is approximately one-twenty-ninth of the United States' total land area (3,537,441 square miles). Fittingly, the state motto is "Crescit Eundo," or "It Grows as It Goes."**

The Zía sun design featured on the flag comes from a water jar discovered at Zía Pueblo. This pueblo is thought to have been one of the Seven Golden Cities of Cíbola, so desperately sought by Spanish explorer Vásquez de Coronado. The sun symbol reflects the Zía philosophy of the basic harmony of the universe. Four is the sacred number of the Zía, representing the earth's four directions; the four seasons of the year; the four points of the day (sunrise, noon, evening, and night); the four divisions of life (childhood, youth, adulthood, and old age); and the four sacred obligations (strong body, clear mind, pure spirit, and devotion to the welfare of others). All of these things are bound together in the circle of life; thus, the circle at the heart of the sun.

> **The chile and the frijole (pinto bean) are New Mexico's two state vegetables.**

The flag's bold red and yellow were the colors of Spain's Queen Isabella, who is remembered for sponsoring the exploration of much of the New World. It was under flags of red and yellow that Spanish conquistadors first sailed to the New World, eventually making their way through New Spain (soon to become Mexico) and into the American Southwest. The Spaniards' main interest in the New World was gold. Just as this precious ore would later bring American pioneers to the Wild West, it brought Spaniards in earlier centuries.

Although few would guess it, New Mexico's capital is the oldest of any capital city in the United States. The Spanish founded Santa Fe, originally named *La Villa Real de la Santa Fe de San Francisco de Asis*, in 1609. The city was built on prehistoric Native American ruins.

New Mexico state statute describes the sun symbol's proportions on the flag as four groups of sun rays set at right angles with the two inner sun rays one-fifth longer than the two outer rays. The diameter of the circle in the center of the sun is one-third the width of the entire symbol. New Mexico also has an "Official Salute to the Flag." In English, it is as follows: "I salute the flag of the State of New Mexico and the Zía symbol of perfect friendship among united cultures." In Spanish, it reads: *"Saludo la bandera del estado de Nuevo Méjico, el simbolo Zía de amistad perfecta, entre culturas unidas."* This salute was composed by several women from the Portales Chapter of the United Daughters of the Confederacy. The English version was adopted by the state's 26th Legislature on March 13, 1963. The Spanish version, translated by schoolteacher Maria E. Naranjo of Santa Fe, was adopted by the 31st Legislature in 1973.

In the "Great NAVA Survey of 2001," Dr. Mera's flag design ranked first out of seventy-two flags from Canada and the United States! The four hundred thirty-seven flag enthusiasts who voted chose the yellow and red flag of New Mexico for its simplicity and symbolism, its distinctness and color. This flag is truly an American beauty.

The Rio Grande river runs through the middle of New Mexico; to the south it serves as the border between Texas and Mexico. The Rio Grande is approximately 1,885 miles long and originates in the Rocky Mountains of Colorado. At its mouth the river drains into the Gulf of Mexico.

Despite the state's reputation of intense heat and desert lands, there actually are cotton farms in New Mexico. They are located along the Rio Grande and Pecos Rivers.

Arizona

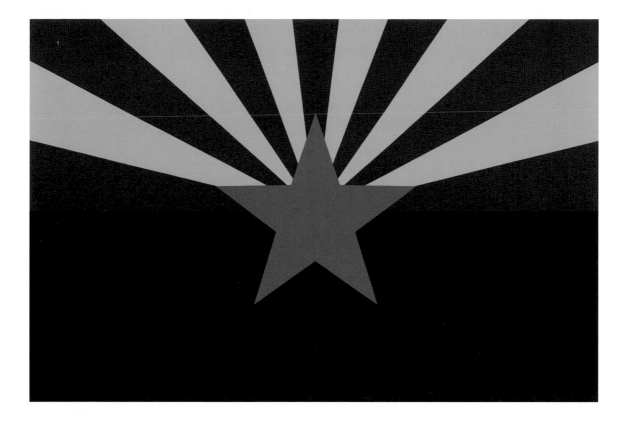

Arizona

Admitted

February 14, 1912

"Come to this land of sunshine/To this land where life is young/Where the wide, wide world is waiting/The songs that will now be sung/Where the golden sun is flaming/Into warm, white shining day/And the sons of men are blazing/Their priceless right of way." So goes the first verse of "Arizona," written by Margaret R. Clifford.

It seems appropriate, both weather-wise and vexillologically, to have two references to the sun in Arizona's state song. During the month of July, the temperatures range, on average, from 70 degrees to 106 degrees Fahrenheit. And on the state's flag you will find rays of light in red and gold. Symbolically, this makes sense because when people think of Arizona, they usually think of the sun.

In the late 1800s, the trend of simply embroidering the state seal upon a field of blue began to fade. Wyoming was the first to hint at this—their state seal appeared as a brand on a large white bison—and after Utah, no other state would employ its seal on a flag. Oklahoma paid tribute to its Native American population with a war shield and instruments of peace. New Mexico also referenced its Native American roots; it placed the sun symbol of the Zía tribe upon a field of yellow. Arizona, our forty-eighth state, was next in line with a creative flag design of its own.

In 1908, four years after adopting a forty-six-star flag for the nation, the United States had to make another change. Two more states, New Mexico and Arizona, had joined the Union. Since there were now forty-eight states, it was only appropriate that the nation's flag have forty-eight stars. The new flag was signed into law in 1912, and "Old Glory" would not be updated again until after Alaska and Hawaii were granted statehood.

Robert G. Heft designed the current American flag while he was still a high school student, in 1959. The United States Congress adopted this new fifty-star flag on July 4, 1960, and Heft would go on to be the mayor of a town in Ohio.

In 1910, during the National Rifle Matches at Camp Perry in Ohio, members of the Arizona Rifle Team noticed that all the other state rifle teams had flags. They suggested to Colonel Charles W. Harris, the adjutant general of the Arizona National Guard, that a state flag be created. Colonel Harris went to Nan Hayden (the wife of U.S. Congressman Carl Hayden) for help, and they quickly got to work.

In a move that would surely please the Flagman, Harris and Hayden considered how to design the flag symbolically, in a historical context. Next they considered colors. Spanish conquistadors led by Vásquez de Coronado, in their 1540 expedition through what would become Arizona to find the Seven Cities of Cibola, carried the colors red and gold. Arizona's state colors are blue and gold. So Harris and Hayden chose blue, for loyalty, as well as red and "old gold," for Arizona's sun. (The gold color is referred to as both "old gold" and "yellow." This is true of the New Mexico flag as well.) Mrs. Hayden sewed the flag and on February 17, 1917, the Arizona State Legislature adopted her Copper Star Flag.

> Arizona experienced an incredible jump in population between 1990 and 2000. According to the 2000 census, 5,130,632 call the state home, an increase of 40 percent! The population increase in the United States was 13.1 percent during this time.

This new state flag was described in Chapter 7 of the Session Laws of Arizona. "The flag of the State of Arizona shall be as follows: The lower half of the flag shall be a blue field; the upper half shall be divided into thirteen equal segments, or rays, which shall start at the center on the lower line and continue to the edges of the flag. . . . In the center of the flag, superimposed, a copper colored five-point star" is placed so that the uppermost point is one foot from the top of the flag and the lower points are one foot from the bottom. "The red and blue shall be of the same shades as the colors in the flag of the United States."

Arizona is the country's largest producer of copper, so the flag's star is the color of copper. The bottom half of this star rests on the field of blue. The top half fits nicely, angles and all, into the upper half of the flag. The thirteen rays of the sun, representing the thirteen colonies, dominate the top half of the flag. It was thought that the rays of the setting sun were appropriate for a western state.

Arizona has had just the one flag since the adoption of the Copper Star Flag, five years after President William Howard Taft signed Congress's Act of Admission. Arizona is known as the "Valentine State" because it was granted statehood on February 14, 1912. It was the last of the continental states to join the Union.

> **Arizona has actually chosen to name an official neckwear. The honor goes . . . to the bola tie! The official bola is silver with a turquoise pendant.**

> **Just south of Utah's amazing national parks, Zion and Bryce Canyons, is Arizona's number-one tourist attraction, the Grand Canyon. Considered one of the "Seven Natural Wonders of the World," this fine specimen of erosion is almost 300 miles long and 2,000 total square miles.**
>
> **The area was granted national park status in 1919. Millions of people have arrived, ever since, to take in the scenery, hike, shoot the rapids of the Colorado River, ride mules and horses, or take helicopter trips over the Grand Canyon.**

Alaska

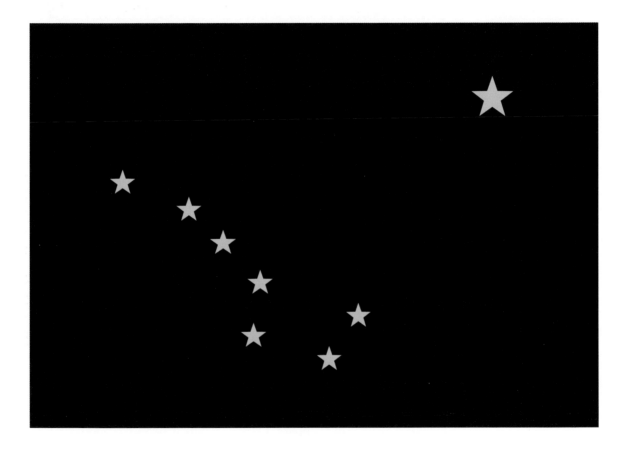

Alaska

Admitted

January 3, 1959

Alaska is almost one-fifth the size of the entire United States. Most scholars believe that the first Native Americans came to North America from Siberia, traveling across Alaska back when North America and Asia were connected by land. (Today Alaska and Russia are separated by a narrow strip of water called the Bering Strait.)

In March 1867, Secretary of State William H. Seward agreed to purchase Alaska from Russia. People were skeptical of the move, especially with a price tag of $7,200,000. At the time Seward was mocked by many; when not referring to Alaska as "Icebergia," critics called it "Seward's Folly."

Those Americans daring enough to move to this far-off region quickly developed a fishing industry. However, as in California and Nevada, it was gold that really gave the area a boost. The year 1896 marked the beginning of Alaska's Klondike Gold Rush; ten years later, Alaska had attracted enough people, and attention, to be granted a representative in the United States Congress. In 1912, Alaska gained official recognition as a territory. The next step was statehood. But first, a flag.

In 1926, the Alaska Department of the American Legion set out to find the territory a symbol. They arranged a flag contest, but with a twist: the contest was limited to Alaskan children enrolled in grades seven through twelve. The

> **The World Eskimo Indian Olympics is an annual event that includes the "Seal Hop," a game of endurance (contestants hop, using their feet and knuckles, while in the push-up position), the "Four Man Carry" (which mimics the carrying of the kill after a hunt), the "Ear Pull" (two people face off with twine looped around each other's ear and play tug-of-war), and the "*Nalakatuk*" (or "Blanket Toss"), in which participants use walrus skins to toss a volunteer into the air, sometimes as high as thirty feet. At Christmas, these jumping volunteers throw candy to children. The final event of the WEIO is the naming of Miss Top of the World. The Eskimo, Athabascan, Tsimshian, Haida, Tlingit, and Aleut tribes are included on the Olympic rings design that is used to promote the games.**

flag committee rejected several designs, including a polar bear on an iceberg, because they represented only one region of Alaska. The winning entry, designed by thirteen-year-old John Bell (Benny) Benson, was a simple pattern of eight gold stars on a field of dark blue. At the time of the contest, Benny Benson was living in an orphanage in Seward, Alaska. For his winning design, he was awarded a $1,000 scholarship, a gold watch with an engraving of his flag design, and a trip to Washington, D.C., to present the new Alaska flag to President Calvin Coolidge. Although Benny never did make the trip to Washington, his flag was adopted by the Territorial Legislature in May of 1927.

> **Benny Benson's flag design earned Alaska a fifth place finish in the "Great NAVA Survey of 2001." When it comes to land, though, Alaska is second to none. At 586,400 square miles, Alaska is twice the size of Texas.**

Benny's flag was not only aesthetically appealing, it was symbolic. He chose the dark blue field as a tribute to both the Alaskan sky and the forget-me-not (which was named state flower in 1949). Of the nine stars, one stands apart from the others and is larger in size. This represents the North Star. Benny chose it as a symbol for his territory, which he was sure would soon be the northernmost state in the United States. The remaining stars form the Big Dipper (which is not actually a constellation but an "asterism," a distinct group of stars). The Big Dipper's handle is also the tail of the constellation Ursa Major, or Great Bear; the Big Dipper's cup is the Great Bear's flank. Benny included the Great Bear in his flag to symbolize strength.

In 1959, when Alaska was granted statehood, Benny's flag became the official state flag. Today in Anchorage you will find Benny Benson Boulevard as well as an alternative secondary school named in his honor. Another tribute was paid to Benny Benson on January 17, 2002, at the opening of the Alaska State Museum exhibit to commemorate the seventy-fifth anniversary of the adoption of the Alaskan flag. "Benny Benson made a tremendous impact on Alaska history when he submitted his entry that featured the Big Dipper and the North Star," Lt. Governor Fran Ulmer said. "His story is a wonderful example of how one young person can really make a difference. The flag story continues to remind us of the importance of listening to the ideas and opinions of young people."

In 1935, Marie Drake, an employee of the Alaska Department of Education, wrote a poem called "Alaska's Flag" as part of a newsletter story on Benny Benson. Composer Elinor Dusenbury set the poem to music and the Territorial Legislature adopted "Alaska's Flag" as the state song in 1955. Its final verse is: "The great North Star with its steady light/Over land and sea a beacon bright/Alaska's flag—to Alaskans dear/The simple flag of a last frontier."

The last frontier is still thriving today. Although the state ranks last in the nation in farming, it leads in commercial fishing. Alaska contains great oil reserves, and its natural beauty draws hundreds of cruise ships every year. There is much to be seen here, much more than just a polar bear on an iceberg.

Alaska adopted "North to the Future" as its state motto during the Alaska Purchase Centennial in 1967. The words were first written by Richard Peter, a newsman from Juneau, who says that the motto "is a reminder that beyond the horizon of urban clutter there is a Great Land beneath our flag that can provide a new tomorrow for this century's 'huddled masses yearning to breathe free.'"

Hawaii

Hawaii

Admitted

August 21, 1959

Captain James Cook was the first European to set foot on Hawaii. After his accidental arrival, in 1778, more Brits followed. Therefore, Hawaii's flag is loosely based on a flag that flew overhead long ago: the upper left canton of the flag closely resembles Great Britain's "Union Jack." Hawaii's flag also features eight red, white, and blue stripes to represent the state's eight major islands.

The Hawaiian flag has been the flag of a kingdom, a republic, a United States territory, and a state. Before 1810, each of the Hawaiian Islands had its own king. The first ruler to unify all the Hawaiian Islands was King Kamehameha. Other than some minor skirmishes, King Kamehameha met with very little resistance as he organized Hawaii (without benefit of a written language) and established Hawaii Island as the capital of this "nation." In 1816, King Kamehameha commissioned the creation of the Hawaiian flag. To this day, King Kamehameha is celebrated all across the state on June 11.

In 1843, King Kamehameha's grandson, King Kamehameha III, had his power seized by Great Britain's Lord Paulette, a move that had not been approved by the British monarchy. King Kamehameha III regained control five months later and proclaimed, *"Ua mau ke ea o ka 'aina i ka pono"*: "The life of the land is perpetuated in righteousness." Eventually these words would become Hawaii's state motto. King Kamehameha III continued to rely heavily on his British advisors, and Hawaii remained a sovereign kingdom until 1893, when a group of American businessmen and John L. Stevens, an American minister, took the power away from the monarchy. The businessmen were interested in Hawaii's sugar plantations, and the Dole family had set its sights on the island's pineapple farms. (Hawaii would soon supply one-third of the world's pineapples.) A treaty of reciprocity had been signed in 1875 and it

In 1993, President Bill Clinton signed the Apology Resolution, "To acknowledge the 100th anniversary of the January 17, 1893 overthrow of the Kingdom of Hawaii, and to offer an apology to Native Hawaiians on behalf of the United States for the overthrow of the Kingdom of Hawaii."

brought money and jobs to the Islands. It also brought trouble, however, as tension mounted between the Hawaiians and the Americans.

In 1889, native Hawaiians revolted, displaying their unhappiness with the constitution that had been forced on the reigning monarch, King Kalakaua. The Americans were able to stifle the rebellion, and four years later a temporary government, referred to as the Committee of Safety, was assembled as these Americans declared an end to the monarchy. Minister Stevens declared that Hawaii was no longer a country but a United States protectorate, but President Grover Cleveland refused to annex (or seize) Hawaii. He even tried to restore Queen Lili`uokalani, but the revolutionary Committee of Safety refused to give up their power. Instead, on July 4, 1894, they declared the island to be a republic and named San-

Nickname

"Aloha State"

Motto

"The Life of the Land Is Perpetuated in Righteouness"

ford B. Dole as the president. On June 14, 1900, Hawaii was finally made a United States territory and Dole, a cousin of the pineapple magnates, was named the governor.

Along with its natural beauty and bountiful sugar cane and pineapples, Hawaii has a strategic location in the Pacific Ocean. The United States Navy quickly established a headquarters at Pearl Harbor in 1908. Despite the controversies of the recent past, many Hawaiians now seemed eager for statehood. This only increased after the December 7, 1941, attack on Pearl Harbor and the United States' subsequent defeat of Japan in World War II. John A. Burns, Hawaii's representative in Congress, put together the deal for statehood, and President Dwight D. Eisenhower signed the Act of Admission on March 18, 1959. Hawaii was admitted as the fiftieth state in August of that year, and in 1960 the United States adopted its fifty-star flag.

There are still those who want independence for Hawaii. As in Vermont, these secessionists desire a government with no attachment to the United States, even if that government is a monarchy. These Hawaiians even refer to their state status as an illegal military occupation. "It took Britain only five months to withdraw from its unlawful colonial occupation. Why must it take the U.S. over a century to go home?" asks Dr. Kekuni Blaisdell, a leader of the Indigenous Rights Movement in the Pacific. The Hawaiian Kingdom, the monarchy that cannot rule within the American democratic system, went so far as to file a complaint with the United Nations. On July 5, 2001, David Keanu Sai, Acting Minister of the Interior and the Chairman of the Council of Regency (associated with the Hawaiian Kingdom), went to New York City in the name of his homeland. The complaint was filed against the United States in accordance with Article 35(2) of the United Nations Charter: "A State which is not a Member of the United Nations may bring to the attention of the Security Council or of the General Assembly any dispute to which it is a party if it accepts in advance, for the purpose of the dispute, the obligations of pacific settlement provided in the present Charter." The U.N. Security Council has yet to act on this complaint.

> **With a population of 1,211,537 people, Hawaii is the ninth-smallest state in the nation. It is also the eighth-smallest state, land-wise, with a total area of 10,932 square miles.**

Meanwhile, these activists continue their pursuit of freedom. Just as Native Americans fought futilely against the pioneers and the United States Army, and just as colonists fought successfully against the monarchy of Great Britain, there are those who do not wish to be a part of the fifty states. In the words of Lili`uokalani, the last reigning queen of Hawaii, "The cause of Hawaii and independence is larger and dearer than the life of any man connected with it. Love of country is deep-seated in the breast of every Hawaiian, whatever his station."